Connecticut

Mapping the Nutmeg State through History

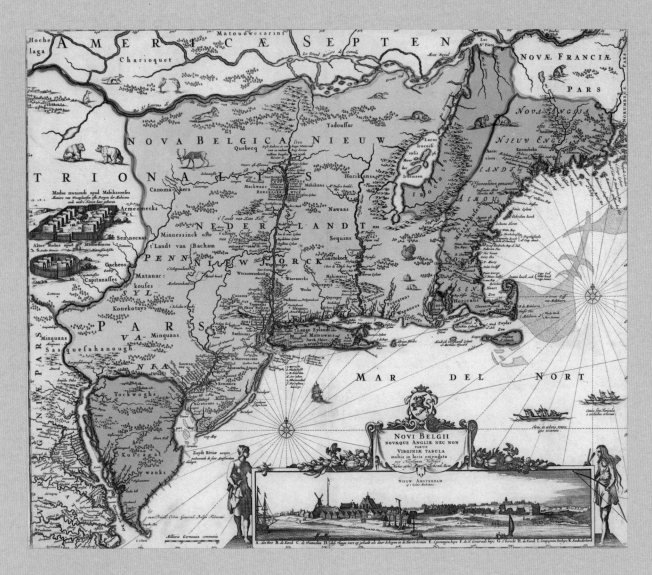

Novi Belgii Novæque Angliæ : nec non partis Virginiæ tabula multis in locis emendata—
Visscher nunc apud Iun (ca. 1690)

How quickly English settlers spread across "Connittekock" is clear from this late-seventeenth-century map of New England. Towns stretch along the coast of Long Island Sound from the modern border with New York State to east of the Connecticut River (still identified by the name "Versche" given to it by Adriaen Block in 1614) and up the river itself.

Dutch cartographer Nicholaes Visscher rendered the English settlements' names phonetically with varying degrees of accuracy: "Gilfort" for Guilford and "Hertfort" for Hartford, but "Zeebroeck" for Saybrook and "Weeters Velt" for Wethersfield. Areas occupied by native peoples, including the "Pequotoos" (Pequots) and the "Moricans" (Mohegans) are noted as well. Adrift in the sea of English settlement is the Dutch trading post "Forte de Goede Hoop" (House of Good Hope). The European who first sailed up the Connecticut River is commemorated by "Adriaen Blocks Eylant," today's Block Island.

Connecticut

MAPPING THE NUTMEG STATE THROUGH HISTORY

Vincent Virga

and Diana Ross McCain

Globe
Pequot

Guilford, Connecticut

Globe Pequot

An imprint of The Rowman & Littlefield Publishing Group, Inc.
4501 Forbes Blvd., Ste. 200
Lanham, MD 20706
www.rowman.com

Distributed by NATIONAL BOOK NETWORK

British Library Cataloguing in Publication Information available

The hardback edition of this book was previously cataloged by the Library of Congress as follows:

Library of Congress Cataloging-in-Publication Data

Virga, Vincent.
Connecticut, mapping the Nutmeg State through history : rare and unusual maps from the Library of Congress / Vincent Virga and Diana Ross McCain.
p. cm.
ISBN 978-0-7627-6005-3
1. Connecticut—Maps. 2. Historical geography—Connecticut—Maps. 3. Atlases.
I. McCain, Diana Ross. II. Title.
G1240.V6 2011
911'.746—dc22

ISBN 978-1-4930-3717-9 (paperback)
ISBN 978-0-7627-6748-9 (e-book)
ISBN 978-0-7627-6005-3 (hardback)

∞™ The paper used in this publication meets the minimum requirements of American National Standard for Information Sciences—Permanence of Paper for Printed Library Materials, ANSI/NISO Z39.48-1992

Printed in the United States of America

Contents

Foreword

FIFTY MILES BY NINETY MILES? WHEN I LIVED IN New Haven, I could have cycled the length and width of the state on spring and fall weekends! No wonder the bigger colonies balked when the Articles of Confederation (1777) proposed state equality: One vote for each member? Fifty by ninety? In 1787 the Connecticut delegates artfully proposed The Connecticut Compromise (or The Great Compromise). Each state received an equal vote in the second branch of the legislature, while seats in the first branch were based on population. Diana Ross McCain wisely praises Connecticut's "ingenious entrepreneurs." They later married innovative ideas to geography, transforming the state from an agriculture-based economy in 1830 to a manufacturing powerhouse in 1900. With its maps visualizing social power, Connecticut became first among equals.

Living on planet Earth has always raised certain questions from those of us so inclined. Of course, the most obvious one is: Where am I? Well, as Virginia Woolf sagely noted in her diary, writing things down makes them more real; this may have been a motivating factor for the Old Stone Age artists who invented the language of signs on the walls of their caves in southern France and northern Spain between 37,000 and 11,000 years ago. Picasso reportedly said, "They've invented everything," which includes the very concept of an image.

A map is an image. It makes the world more real for us and uses signs to create an essential sense of place in our imagination. (The petroglyphic maps that were inscribed in the late Iron Age on boulders high in the Valcamonica region of northern Italy are early examples of such signs.) Cartographic imaginings not only locate us on this Earth but also help us invent our personal and social identities since maps embody our social order. Like the movies, maps helped create our national identity—though cinema had a vastly wider audience—and this encyclopedic series of books aims to make manifest the changing social order that invented the United States, which is why it embraces all fifty states.

Each map is a precious link in the chain of events that is the history of our "great experiment," the first and enduring federal government ingeniously deriving its just powers—as Thomas Jefferson proposed—from the consent of the governed. Each state has a physical presence that holds a unique place in any representation of our republic in maps. To see each one rise from the body of the continent conjures Tom Paine's excitement over the resourcefulness, the fecundity, the creative energy of our Enlightenment philosopher-founders: "We are brought at once to the point of seeing government begin, as if we had lived in the beginning of time." Just as the creators systemized not only laws but also rights in our constitution, so our maps show how their collective memory inspired the body politic to organize, codify, classify all of Nature to do their bidding with passionate preferences state by state. For they knew, as did Alexander Pope:

> All are but parts of one
> stupendous Whole
> Whose body Nature is,
> and God the soul.

And aided by the way maps under interrogation often evoke both time and space, we editors and historians have linked the reflective historical overviews of our nation's genesis to the seduction of place embedded in the art and science of cartography.

On October 9, 1492, after sailing westward for four weeks in an incomprehensibly vast and unknown sea, an anxious Christopher Columbus spotted an unidentified flock of migrating birds flying south and signifying land—"Tierra! Tierra!" Changing course to align his ships with this overhead harbinger of salvation, he avoided being drawn into the northern-flowing Gulf Stream, which was waiting to be charted by Ben Franklin around the time our eagle became America as art. And so, on October 11, Columbus encountered the salubrious southern end of San Salvador. Instead of somewhere in the future New England, he came up the lee of the island's west coast to an easy and safe anchorage.

Lacking maps of the beachfront property before his eyes, he assumed himself in Asia because in his imagination there were only three parts to the known world: Europe, Asia, and Africa. To the day he died, Columbus doubted he had come upon a fourth part even though Europeans had already begun appropriating through the agency of maps what to them was a New World, a new continent. Perhaps the greatest visual statement of the general confusion that rocked the Old World as word spread of Columbus's interrupted journey to Asia is the Ruysch map of 1507 (see page viii). Here we see our nascent home inserted into the template created in the second century by Ptolemy, a mathematician, astrologer, and geographer of the Greco-Roman known world, the *oikoumene.*

This map changed my life. It opened my eyes to the power of a true cultural landscape. It taught me that I must always *look* at what I *see* on a map, focusing my attention on why the map was made, not who made it, when or where it was made, but *why.* The Ruysch map was made to circulate the current news. It is a quiet meditative moment in a very busy, noisy time. It is life on the cusp of a new order. And the new order is what Henry Steele Commager christened the "utopian romance" that is America. No longer were maps merely mirrors of nature for me. No longer were the old ones "incorrect" and ignorant of the "truth." No longer did they exist simply to orient me in the practical world. The Ruysch map is reality circa 1507! It is a time machine. It makes the invisible past visible. Blessedly free of impossible abstractions and idealized virtues, it is undeniably my sort of primary historical document.

The same year, 1507, the Waldseemüller map appeared (see page ix). It is yet another reality and one very close to the one we hold dear. There we Americans are named for the first time. And there

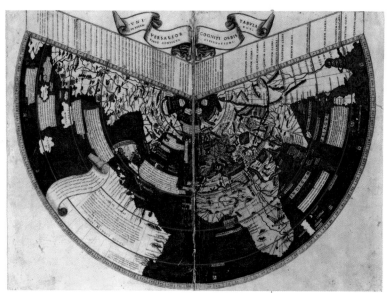

Ruysch map, 1507

we sit, an independent continent with oceans on both sides of us, six years *before* Balboa supposedly discovered "the other sea." There are few maps as mysterious for cartographic scholars as Wald-seemüller's masterpiece. Where did all that news come from? For our purposes it is sufficient to say to the world's visual imagination, "Welcome to us Americans in all our cartographic splendor!"

Throughout my academic life, maps were never offered to me as primary historical documents. When I became a picture editor, I learned, to my amazement, that most book editors are logocentric, or "word people." (And thank God! If they weren't, I wouldn't have my career.) Along with most historians and academics, they make their livelihood working with words and ideas. The fact of my being an "author" makes me a word person, too, of course.

But I store information visually, as does a map. (If I ask myself where my keys are, I "see" them in my mind's eye; I don't inform myself of their whereabouts in words.) So I, like everyone who reveres maps as story-tellers, am both a word person and a person who can think in pictures. This is the modus operandi of a map-maker recording the world in images for the visually literate. For a traditional historian, maps are merely archival devices dealing with scientific accuracy. They cannot "see" a map as a first-person, visual narrative crammed with very particular insights to the process of social history. However, the true nature of maps as a key player in the history of the human imagination is a cornerstone of our series.

The very title of this volume, *Connecticut: Mapping the Nutmeg State through History,* makes it clear that this series has a specific agenda, as does each map. It aims to thrust us all into a new intimacy with the American experience by detailing the creative process of our nation in motion through time and space via word *and* image. It grows from the relatively recent shift in consciousness about the physical, mental, and spiritual relevance of maps in our understanding of our lives on Earth. Just as each state is an integral part of the larger United States, "Where are we?" is a piece of the larger puzzle called "Who are we?"

The Library of Congress was founded in 1800 with 740 volumes and three maps. It has grown into the world's largest library and is known as "America's Memory." For me, its vast visual holdings made by those who helped build

Waldseemüller map, 1507

this nation make the Library the eyes of our nation as well. There are nearly five million maps in the Geography and Map Division. We have linked our series with that great collection in the hopes that its astonishing breadth will inspire us in our efforts to strike Lincoln's "mystic chords of memory" and create living history.

On January 25, 1786, Thomas Jefferson wrote to Archibald Stuart, "Our confederacy must be viewed as the nest from which all America, North and South, is to be peopled." This is a man who could not live without books. This is a man who drew maps. This is a politician who, in spite of his abhorrence of slavery and his respect for Native Americans, took pragmatic rather than principled positions when confronted by both "issues." Nonetheless, his bold vision of an expanded American universe informs our current enterprise. There is no denying that the

story of the United States has a dark side. What makes the American narrative unique is the ability we have displayed time and again to remedy our mistakes, to adjust to changing circumstances, to debate, and then move on in new directions that seem better for all.

For Jefferson, whose library was the basis for the current Library of Congress after the British burned the first one during the War of 1812, and for his contemporaries, the doctrine of progress was a keystone of the Enlightenment. The maps in our books are reports on America, and all of their political programs are manifestations of progress. Our starting fresh, free of old-world hierarchies, class attitudes, and the errors of tradition, is wedded to our geographical isolation and its immunity from the endless internal European wars devastating humanity, which justify Jefferson's confessing, "I like the dreams of the future better than the history of the past." But, as the historian Michael Kammen explains, "For much of our history we have been present-minded; yet a usable past has been needed to give shape and substance to national identity." Historical maps keep the past warm with life and immediately around us. They encourage critical inquiry, curiosity, and qualms.

For me, this series of books celebrating each of our states is not about the delineation of property rights. It is a depiction of the pursuit of happiness, which is listed as one of our natural rights in the 1776 Declaration of Independence. (Thirteen years later, when the French revolutionaries drafted a Declaration of the Rights of Man, they included "property rights," and Jefferson unsuccessfully urged them to substitute "pursuit of happiness" for "property.") Jefferson also believed, "The Earth belongs always to the living generation." I believe these books depict what each succeeding generation in its pursuit of happiness accomplished on this portion of the Earth known as the United States. If America is a matter of an idea, then maps are an image of that idea.

I also fervently believe these books will show the states linked in the same way Lincoln saw the statement that all men are created equal as "the electric cord in that Declaration that links the hearts of patriotic and liberty-loving men together, that will link those patriotic hearts as long as the love of freedom exists in the minds of men throughout the world."

VINCENT VIRGA
WASHINGTON, D.C.
2010

Introduction

CONNECTICUT IS A COMPACT STATE. THE DISTANCE between the shoreline that is its southern boundary and its northern border with Massachusetts is around just 50 miles. From New York State on its western edge to Rhode Island on the east is only about 90 miles. Connecticut's area of approximately 5,000 square miles makes it the third smallest of the fifty states, ranking ahead of only Delaware and Rhode Island.

Yet within this rough rectangle of land there is a surprising range of geographic features. Connecticut is not a land of extremes, but of variety.

The state boasts no significant natural resources—no mines of precious gems or of valuable ore, no deposits of coal. There is only the land. It is strikingly beautiful, but from the very beginning it has challenged its people to make the best of it with hard work and ingenuity.

Long Island Sound constitutes Connecticut's entire southern border. The 98-mile coastline is irregular, with dozens of inlets, some large enough to have served as harbors for large sailing ships. The shoreline is picturesquely rocky, with few stretches of sandy beach.

Hundreds of islands are scattered in the waters off the coastline. Some are big enough to hold a lighthouse or a small neighborhood of houses, while others are barely bumps that vanish when the tide is high.

The biggest island off the Connecticut coast is Long Island. It parallels the entire Connecticut shoreline, with the two bodies of land being no more than 20 miles apart at any point. On a clear day a person standing on the Connecticut shore can see Long Island on the horizon.

Long Island acts as a buffer for Connecticut. It is one of the reasons the state's beaches typically lack powerful surf. But Long Island also has at times protected Connecticut from the worst of weather, absorbing much of the force of strong storms and even hurricanes before they reach its neighbor to the north.

Several broad rivers flow serenely through valleys to empty into Long Island Sound. The longest, the Connecticut River, cuts roughly north and south through the entire middle of the state. The lands on either side of these waterways are typically fertile, easily tillable acres.

The first English to arrive in Connecticut in the 1600s settled along the coastline and the major river valleys, which offered significant advantages for the period. Water was the easiest and most efficient way to travel and move goods during the seventeenth century. The harbors served as ports for sailing vessels that traded with coastal communities and as far as the West Indies. Rivers and Sound alike provided what today would be considered a phenomenal abundance and variety of fish and shellfish that could be consumed locally or preserved and shipped out. And the land in the valleys was the best Connecticut had to offer.

Away from the coast and river valleys, the land, while still productive, becomes hillier, rougher, and rockier. Settlers moved into these areas only as land in the river valleys was taken up. The next region of Connecticut to be settled, after the river valleys and coast, was the northeastern portion of the state, starting at the turn of the eighteenth century. The land here is hillier, making cultivation more difficult.

Finally, in the mid-1700s, settlement moved into the most rugged portion of the state, the northwestern corner. While the hills in the northeastern section might rise to 1,000 feet at most, those in the northwest can be twice as tall. Some of these steep-sided peaks merit the term "mountain."

An additional challenge to settlers in the areas away from the river valleys was the fact that much of the land was riddled with stones, ranging in size from small rocks to boulders, that had to be cleared from fields before cultivation could begin. Clearing stones was a chore that had to be repeated, since the freezing and thawing of the earth forced more rocks to the surface every year. The Connecticut farmer put these annoying rocks to good use, building stone walls that marked property lines and kept livestock and crops apart. Thousands of miles of stone walls survive today, testimony to the determination and inventiveness of those early farmers.

Eventually the land could not provide a living for a growing population. For more than half a century, from before the American Revolution to the early 1800s, tens of thousands of people left Connecticut in hopes of finding opportunity on frontiers from Vermont to New York to Ohio, and far beyond. Connecticut became the land left behind.

But just as the land had challenged farmers to wrest a living from it, the ultimate inability of the land to support a large agricultural population challenged those who did not emigrate to conceive of new ways to make a livelihood. They developed innovative ways of making products, everything from silk to rubber, from pistols to silverware, faster, more efficiently, and cheaper. And they found an important advantage in the Connecticut landscape.

In the northeastern portion of the state, and even more significantly in the northwestern, are an abundance of streams. Their swift waters cascade over rocky courses, creating striking waterfalls and, as occupants also came to appreciate, significant sources of power to operate factories.

Waterways remained the most efficient means of transportation for the first two centuries of Connecticut history. But they were superseded in the middle of the 1800s by the railroad. Some tracks paralleled the rivers and shoreline, but others were laid out to locations far from a navigable waterway. These new transportation connections opened up many towns to the world.

The railroad provided a powerful impetus to Connecticut manufacturing. Trains also inaugurated the development of shoreline towns and some inland communities as vacation destinations for city dwellers.

Connecticut factories needed workers. The answer came in the form of tens of thousands of immigrants from more than two dozen European countries. By the turn of the twentieth century, Connecticut was a predominantly urban industrial state, with one of the most diverse populations in the United States.

Another transportation innovation remade Connecticut in the twentieth century. Automobiles, and the thousands of miles of roads built to accommodate them, changed the meaning of distance and time for the average individual. Lives were no longer regulated by train timetables or limited by the extent of tracks.

The post-war baby boom and the availability of inexpensive transportation entirely under the individual's control led to the rise of the suburbs. Suburbs spread across the face of Connecticut, transforming small towns and villages into bustling bedroom communities seemingly overnight. Thousands of acres of farmland were converted to home lots. Schools were built to accommodate the expanding number of children. Suburbanization proceeded with a momentum of such strength that it damaged the historic fabric of many small towns and parts of the rural landscape. Sprawl became an important issue in the latter decades of the twentieth century.

At the same time the major cities saw their populations decline, as many of the factories that had been the bedrock of the state's economy for a century, and that had employed thousands, fell victim to cheap competition in other states and high energy costs. Some of the manufacturing jobs were replaced by employees who worked in the many corporate headquarters that relocated to Connecticut, in higher education, and in such enterprises as pharmaceutical research.

The automobile was a boon for one Connecticut industry: tourism. Connecticut's rural landscape had always had its admirers, including artists who had found in it inspiration for great art. Now increasing numbers of tourists came via automobile, seeking the town greens, steepled meetinghouses, and saltboxes of earlier, less hectic times in history. Towns that had been bypassed by the railroad and the juggernaut of industrialization suddenly found themselves appealing as enclaves of relatively untouched history. The small, somewhat unspoiled towns and rural acres of western Connecticut became extremely popular among actors, artists, writers, and celebrities, who could make the trip to New York City by commuter train or car in two or three hours.

As far back as the 1700s, Connecticut was known as the "Land of Steady Habits" for its custom of reelecting the same men to political office year after year. But history has shown that perhaps the steadiest habit in the Connecticut character has been the ability to adapt, to fashion a life from the land in response to repeated, profound changes.

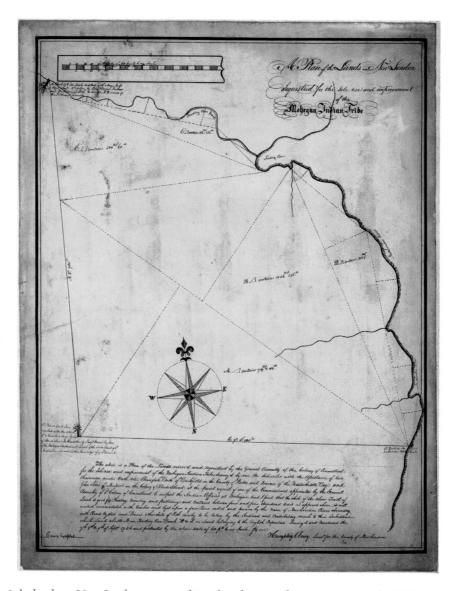

A plan of the lands in New London sequestred for the sole use and improvement of the Mohegan Indian tribe—Survey'd and measured the 7th, 8th & 9th of Septr. 1736 and protracted by the above scale of 60 pts. to an inch by me, Humphry Avery, survr, for the county of New London

A few of Connecticut's native tribes were able to retain possession of at least a portion of their ancestral lands in the generations following the arrival of European settlers. One of these was the Mohegan tribe. The Connecticut legislature in 1736 set aside this area of "between four and five thousand acres" in the town of Montville, surveyed by Humphrey Avery, "for the sole use and improvement" of the Mohegan tribe. Two of the reference points for the survey are black oak trees with piles of stones.

First Encounters

DUTCH TRADER ADRIAEN BLOCK AND THE CREW OF his vessel the *Onrust (Restless)* were the first Europeans to view anything beyond the coastline of what today is Connecticut. In the spring of 1614, Block navigated his ship from the salt water of Long Island Sound north into what he called the "Versch" or "Fresh" River. He may have sailed as far as 60 miles up the river, where he would have encountered the shallow, rough stretch of water known as the Enfield Rapids that would stymie ship captains for the next two centuries.

When Adriaen Block ventured up the "Fresh" River and two others that flow from interior Connecticut into Long Island Sound, the Housatonic and the Thames, the land had been occupied by human beings for at least 10,000 years. Block observed communities of people along the banks of all three rivers he explored. They were, in fact, what he was seeking, for his mission was to identify the potential for the Dutch to trade with native peoples for the beaver pelts highly valued by Europeans.

The native peoples called Block's "Fresh" River the Connecticut, which in their language meant "long, tidal river." This refers to the fact that the rise and fall of the tide can be observed as far north up the river as the Enfield Rapids.

An estimated 30,000 individuals were living in Connecticut at the time of Adriaen Block's visit. While they shared a common lifestyle based on farming, fishing, and hunting, and their languages were similar in many ways, they were not a single united people. More than a dozen different tribes occupied various sections of the state. The Nipmuks and Mohegans lived in the northeastern part of modern Connecticut; the Paugussetts and Siwanogs in southwestern Connecticut; the Quinnipiacs around New Haven; the Tunxis, Podunk, and Poquinock Indians in the area around present-day Hartford; the Pequots in the southeastern corner.

The various tribes did not always coexist harmoniously. They engaged in power struggles over access to resources and trade.

The Dutch were back by 1633 to establish a trading station they called the "House of Good Hope" on the western bank of the Connecticut River at what today is Hartford. But tragedy had struck the population Block had observed during his visit less than two decades earlier, in the form of diseases from Europe to which the native peoples had never before been exposed, and to which they thus had no natural resistance. The worst was smallpox, which had spread from European settlers in Massachusetts to the native peoples there. It didn't take long for the highly infectious disease to make its way from the native peoples of Massachusetts to Connecticut, where more than half of the population died in the course of just a few years.

English Puritans from Massachusetts arrived at the Connecticut River hard on the heels of the Dutch traders, and in far larger numbers. In the 1630s permanent English settlements were established at Hartford, Windsor, and Wethersfield on the Connecticut River and Saybrook at the river's mouth. The House of Good Hope was under English control by 1653.

The English hadn't been in Connecticut for five years before war broke out with some of the native peoples. The primary foes were the Pequots, who, before the arrival of the English, had exerted powerful influence over a number of other tribes, earning the resentment of several of them.

Blood had been shed between the English and the native peoples, including the Pequots, as early as 1634. Tensions and violence, sometimes deadly, between the English and several tribes escalated over the next few years, as repeated attempts at negotiation failed. In April of 1637 the Pequots launched a surprise attack on individuals working in the fields in Wethersfield, killing at least seven and kidnapping two young women.

Within days of this deadly raid, leaders of the Connecticut and Massachusetts Bay colonies had agreed to join forces in a war against the Pequots. The English received support from the Mohegans, Narragansetts, and several other tribes, while the Pequots counted the Western Nehantic among their allies.

The pivotal event of the war was a nighttime attack in May of 1637 by Connecticut and Massachusetts soldiers and their Native American allies on a fortified Pequot village in southeastern Connecticut. The attackers set the village on fire and shot down any who tried to escape the flames. Most of the estimated seven hundred Pequots, many women and children, were killed.

Some Pequots who managed to escape the attack fled west, with the English and their allies in pursuit. Less than two months later the refugees were caught in a swamp in Fairfield, Connecticut. More were killed, and the few who survived that second fight were forced to become slaves of the English or their Native American allies. The Pequot people were nearly—but not entirely—exterminated.

The threat of Indian attack loomed again in Connecticut in 1675, when members of the Wampanoag tribe in Massachusetts, led by a chief named Philip, went to war against Massachusetts settlers. Connecticut officials advised towns to prepare fortifications against possible attack, a warning acted upon as far south as Middletown. The settlement at Simsbury was abandoned and subsequently burned by Native Americans, but Connecticut was spared the carnage that Massachusetts experienced before King Philip's War ended with the death of the Wampanoag chief himself in 1676.

War, disease, and the steady reduction of their land by governmental action, legal and illegal, whittled down the other Connecticut tribes over the course of the next century. In the late 1700s, Samson Occom, a Mohegan who had converted to Christianity and become a minister, gathered together some survivors of the Mohegan, Pequot, Narragansett, Montauk, Nehantic, and Tunxis tribes who also had converted to Christianity, and led them on a journey to a new home among the Oneida Indians in upstate New York, called Brotherton. Several decades later, these people would move again, to what at last was a permanent home in Brotherton, Wisconsin.

But some Native Americans remained in Connecticut. A handful of Pequots continued to live on a small remnant of their ancestral lands, as did several dozen Mohegans. Their tenacity, and that of generations who came after them, was to have a significant impact on Connecticut at the end of the twentieth century.

Most of the Native Americans who lived in Connecticut when Adriaen Block visited no longer exist as a tribe. But their presence is recorded in the names of hundreds of natural features and locations across the state derived from their languages, such as the Shepaug, Connecticut, Housatonic, Scantic, Coginchaug, Quinnipiac, Shetucket, Hockanum, Mattabbesset, and Niantic Rivers—to name just a few.

The figure of the Indians' fort or palizado in New England and the manner of the [sic]destroying it—
Underhill and Mason (1638)

The facts of the brutal massacre that destroyed a significant portion of the Pequot tribe are depicted in fine detail in this woodcut from Captain John Underhill's *Newes from America*, published in 1638 in London. It illustrates the night of May 26, 1637, when a force of Massachusetts and Connecticut soldiers commanded by Captain Underhill and Captain John Mason, and joined by Mohegan and Narragansett Indians, launched a surprise assault on the Pequot fort in the Mystic section of the town of Groton.

A circular stockade of sharp-pointed tree trunks surrounded the Pequot community. The English and their Native American allies attacked without warning. The assault force encountered such fierce resistance from the fort's occupants that they resorted to setting it on fire. Some Pequots continued to fight to the death in the burning fort. Pequots who tried to escape the flames were cut down with muskets, swords, and bow and arrow.

Most of the Pequot fort's estimated seven hundred occupants, largely women and children, were killed. Underhill wrote that following the attack "so many soules lie gasping on the ground so thicke in some places, that you could hardly passe along."

A map of the colonies in Connecticut and Rhode Island, divided by counties & townships, from best authorities—Kitchin (1758)

The gouge in Connecticut's northern boundary in this 1758 map by cartographer Thomas Kitchin originated in the laziness and ineptness of surveyors hired by the Massachusetts Bay Colony more than a century earlier to lay out its boundary with its neighbor to the south. The surveyors made an error in locating the eastern end of the boundary, which was their starting point. Then, instead of performing the survey overland, they sailed down the Atlantic coast, into Long Island Sound, and up the Connecticut River, until they reached a point that they believed—incorrectly—was the same latitude as their already erroneous starting point.

The boundary line based on this bungled survey ran several miles too far to the south, putting the towns of Suffield, Enfield, Somers, and Woodstock within the borders of Massachusetts. The two colonies bickered and legislated and negotiated over the boundary for generations.

At last, in 1749, the residents of the four towns "seceded" from Massachusetts and were accepted into the Colony of Connecticut. The "best authorities" upon which Kitchin based his map didn't reflect the situation as it stood in 1758 from Connecticut's point of view. While he locates Woodstock in Connecticut, the towns of Enfield, Suffield, and Somers are still in Massachusetts.

Colonial Era

What today is the state of Connecticut originated in three separate, independent frontier entities that merged by treaty or by force within thirty years of their settlement. All three sprang up along waterways, which not only were the easiest and most efficient avenues of travel in the 1600s but also boasted the most fertile land.

In the mid-1630s Puritan dissidents from Massachusetts Bay established three settlements along the western bank of the Connecticut River, roughly 50 miles from where it flows into Long Island Sound. This trio—Windsor, Hartford, and Wethersfield—in 1639 joined together under a common framework of government known as the Fundamental Orders.

The Saybrook Colony was established at the mouth of the Connecticut River in 1635 by a group of English entrepreneurs. In 1638 more discontented Puritans from Massachusetts arrived at the mouth of the Quinnipiac River to form a settlement they called New Haven.

The Saybrook Colony was sold to the Connecticut Colony in 1644. But the New Haven Colony existed as a separate, independent government for nearly a quarter of a century—until momentous events 3,000 miles away opened the way for its ultimate extinction.

When both the Connecticut and New Haven colonies had been settled, England was embroiled in a civil war between Royalists and Puritans that left government officials with no time to concern themselves with what was taking place on the other side of the Atlantic. The execution of King Charles I in 1649 ushered in a decade of rule in England by a Puritan Commonwealth that, naturally sympathetic to its co-religionists in New England, let them continue to manage their governmental affairs without interference.

All this changed in 1660, when the son of the beheaded King Charles I regained the throne as King Charles II. This constituted a crisis for both the Connecticut and New Haven colonies, since neither had any official authority from the crown to settle where they were or to govern themselves. Both colonies planned to make the case for their legitimacy before the crown, but the Connecticut Colony was faster, better funded, and enjoyed the advantage of having diplomatic genius John Winthrop Jr. as its representative to England.

Winthrop secured for the Connecticut Colony a Royal Charter of government, which not only validated Connecticut's right to exist but also granted it a degree of self-government so liberal it made Connecticut all but independent of English control. Connecticut was permitted to elect its own governor and lieutenant governor. The only limitation was that it could not pass any laws that were not in agreement with those of England.

Most important from the mapmaker's point of view was the fact that the Royal Charter of 1662 defined the Connecticut Colony's borders as Massachusetts to the north and Long Island Sound on the south—an area that included the New Haven Colony. Outraged New Haven Colony inhabitants resisted gamely for three years. But in 1665 they at last had to submit to the inevitable and accept absorption into the Connecticut Colony.

King Charles's definition of the boundaries of Connecticut was more generous still. The Charter declared that Connecticut's western boundary was the "western sea"—the Pacific Ocean. No one at that time had the faintest idea of the true 3,000-mile breadth of the North American continent. Nonetheless, Connecticut in coming years would seek to enforce that definition of its boundaries, to both its advantage and sorrow.

Connecticut's northern border with Massachusetts was a subject of discord between the two colonies for nearly two centuries. The source of the disagreement was a survey of the border commissioned in 1642 by Massachusetts. The surveyors were supposed to start at a designated point in the east, then lay out the line westward. However, rather than struggle overland through what was mostly still virgin forest, they decided to sail down the Atlantic coast, into Long Island Sound, then up the Connecticut River to the same latitude as the starting point.

However, the surveyors' calculations were

off, with the result that they placed the border between the two colonies on the Connecticut River approximately eight miles farther south than it actually should have been. This put the towns of Enfield, Suffield, Somers, and Woodstock within Massachusetts.

The two colonies proceeded to repeatedly resurvey the line, negotiate over it, and bicker about it. In the mid-1700s Enfield, Suffield, Somers, and Woodstock formally transferred themselves from the jurisdiction of Massachusetts to that of Connecticut, which had lower taxes. Massachusetts continued to protest a border that lost it four towns, but ultimately in vain.

Settlement in Connecticut initially spread east and west along Long Island Sound, north and south on the Connecticut River, and along other waterways such as the Thames and Housatonic Rivers. Settlement that was any significant distance from the coast not along a waterway proceeded slowly, usually only when the pressure of a growing population and the need for fresh acres necessitated it.

The hillier terrain of northeastern Connecticut began seeing settlers arrive toward the turn of the eighteenth century. As those towns filled up and their lands were parceled out, the most rugged portion of the colony, the northwestern hills, attracted settlers.

Connecticut was settled not by hardy individuals striking out on their own to carve out independent footholds in the wilderness, or by individual entrepreneurs who secured large grants of land from the English crown. For the Puritans who established the colony in the 1600s and dominated it through the 1700s, the concept of community was paramount. The independent congregation of worshipers was the center of society.

The typical process was for several families to leave a settled area for uninhabited acres, which they would clear and begin farming. Puritanism, or Congregationalism as it came to be called, was the established religion of Connecticut. This meant that by law every individual was required to attend Sabbath services at the meetinghouse, as the house of worship was known. Every taxpayer had to pay toward the cost of supporting a Congregational minister and toward the construction and maintenance of the meetinghouse.

For those who lived more than a few miles from the meetinghouse, attending Sunday services was difficult. When a new community of settlers had grown large enough to support its own minister and meetinghouse, it would seek to be established as a separate religious society.

That might eliminate the long trek on Sundays, but participating in civil government still required attending town meetings that were held at the original meetinghouse. Decisions were often made by those who lived closer to the center of town and thus could more conveniently attend meetings and vote. Eventually, residents of a religious society would tire of being underrepresented in local decision-making and would petition to be incorporated as a separate town.

Such bids for independent status were sometimes resisted by the parent town, which did not want to lose the tax revenue being paid by the would-be separatists. But more often than not the appeal for establishment as an individual town would be granted. The names of towns often reflected the residents' English roots—such as Windsor, Kent, Canterbury, and Woodstock—or the Bible that was the foundation of the Puritan faith—such as Bethlehem, Sharon, Goshen, and Canaan.

The difficulty of travel in the colonial era may have accounted, at least in part, for the decision in 1701 to establish New Haven as a co-capital, with Hartford, of Connecticut. From that point on, until well after the Civil War, the Connecticut legislature would meet in Hartford in May and in New Haven in October.

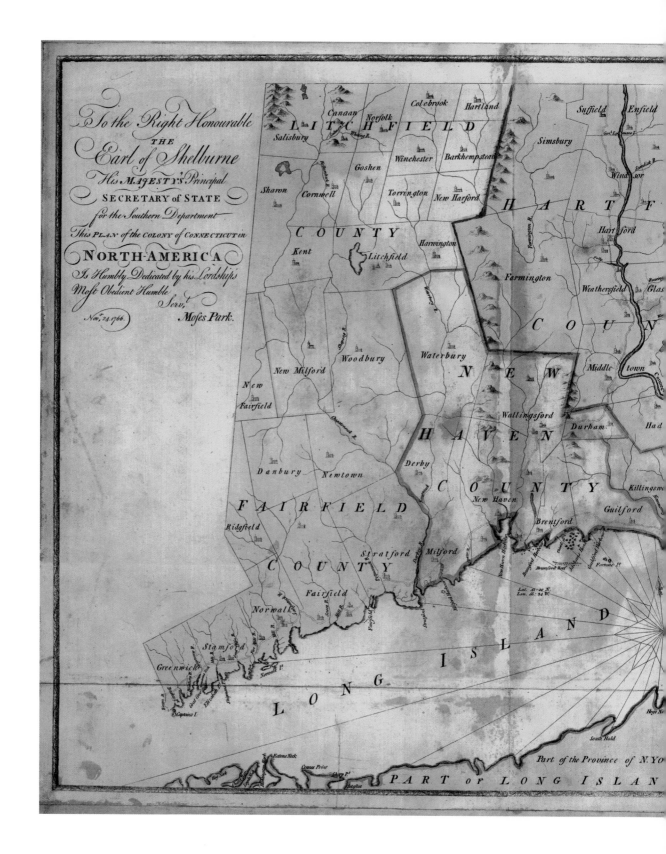

To the Right Honourable
THE
Earl of Shelburne
His MAJESTY'S Principal
SECRETARY of STATE
for the Southern Department
This PLAN of the COLONY of CONNECTICUT in
NORTH-AMERICA
Is Humbly Dedicated by his Lordships
Most Obedient Humble
Serv.t
Nov.r 24. 1766.   Moses Park.

LITCHFIELD

Canaan   Norfolk   Colebrook   Hartland   Suffield   Enfield
Salisbury   Whiting R.   Simsbury   Gen.l Eamore L.
Sharon   Goshen   Winchester   Barkhempstead   Windsor
Cornwell   Torrington   New Harford   HART F
Kent   Harwington   Hartford
COUNTY   Litchfield   Farmington   Weathersfield   Glas
COUN
New Milford   Woodbury   Waterbury   Middletown
New   Fairfield   NEW   Wallingsford   Durham   Had
HAVEN
Danbury   Newtown   Derby   COUNTY   New Haven   Guilford   Killingsw
FAIRFIELD   Brentford
Ridgfield   COUNTY   Stratford   Milford
Fairfield   New Haven Harbour   Lat. 41-14 N.   Fortune I.
Lon. 66: 34 W.
Norwalk   Stamford   Norwalk P.t
Greenwich   LONG ISLAND
Captains I.   Hog Neck   South Hold   Part of the Province of N.YO
Eatons Neck   Crane Point   PART OF LONG ISLAN

24

To the right honourable, the Earl of Shelbourne, His Majesty's principal Secretary of State for the Southern Department.—This plan of the colony of Connecticut in North-America. Is humbly dedicated by his lordship's most obedient humble servt. Moses Park (Novr. 24, 1766)

The entire colony of Connecticut had been settled and organized into towns by the time cartographer Moses Park issued his map in 1766. He also located Suffield, Enfield, and Somers in Connecticut, although Massachusetts would continue to contest the loss of four towns to Connecticut for decades to come, to the confusion of future mapmakers.

The process by which new towns were formed by carving up existing ones was already under way. The first such division occurred in 1692, when the section of the town of "Weathersfield" east of the Connecticut River was incorporated as the town of Glastonbury. Farther south on the Connecticut, the section of the town of "Hadham" that lay east of the river was incorporated in 1734 as the independent town of "East Hadham."

*A new and accurate map of part of North-America,
comprehending the provinces of New England,
New York, Pensilvania, New Jersey, Connecticut,
Rhode Island & part of Virginia, Canada and
Hallifax, for the illustration of Mr. Peter Kalms
travels.—Gibson (1771)*

Suffield, Enfield, and Somers have once again been located in Massachusetts in this 1771 map prepared to illustrate Swedish botanist Peter Kalms's account of his travels in North America.

In the coming decades, Connecticut would press the validity of the Royal Charter of 1662's definition of its western boundary as the "western sea"—the Pacific Ocean. It would lose its claim to the part of northeastern Pennsylvania that fell between the latitudes of Connecticut's northern and southern boundaries when extended westward. But it did not fight for the charter boundary in vain.

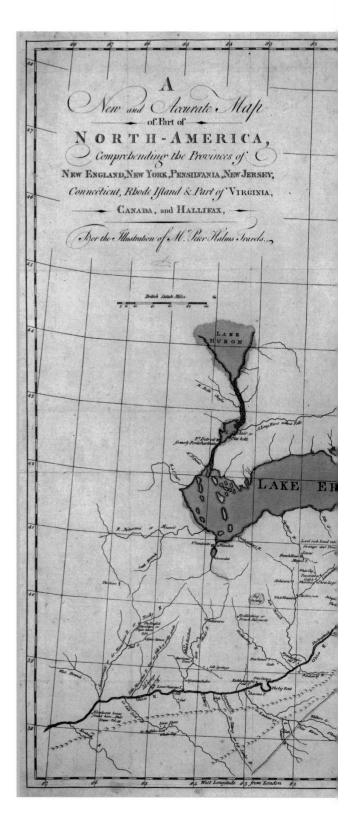

CANADA

LAKE ONTARIO

CANADIAN TERRITORY OF SAGADAHOCK

PROVINCE OF MAIN

NEW HAMP-SHIRE

NEW YORK

PEN SYL VANIA

MASSACHUSETS BAY

RHODE ISLAND

St. George's Bank

VIRGINIA

ATLANTIC

OCEAN

Publish'd according to Act of Parliament March 7th 1771.

17

Nieuwe en nauwkeurige kaart van een gedeelte van Noord Amerika, behelzende Nieuw Engeland, New York, Pensylvania, New Jersey, Connecticut, Rhode Island, een stuk van Virginia, Kanada en Halifax, ter opheldering der reizen van den Heer P. Kalm— Huyser (1772)

In 1786 Connecticut relinquished its claim to any lands past a point 120 miles west of the western border of Pennsylvania. It was allowed to retain title to that 120-mile-wide swath of land between Lake Erie on the north and the latitude of Connecticut's southern border on the south. Connecticut sold the six million acres, an area about the same size as Connecticut itself, to investors in 1795 for a substantial sum, which was put into a fund to support Connecticut's public schools.

The area, known as the Connecticut Western Reserve, was heavily settled by emigrants from Connecticut. It was included in the state of Ohio when it was admitted to the Union in 1803.

HET MEER ONTARIO

CANADA

LANDSTREEK

VAN

SAGADAHOCK

NEW
HAMP-
SHIRE

MASSACHUSETS BAY

RHODE
ISLAND

Jefferys
Bank

St. Georges Bank

ATLANTISCHE

OCEAAN

29

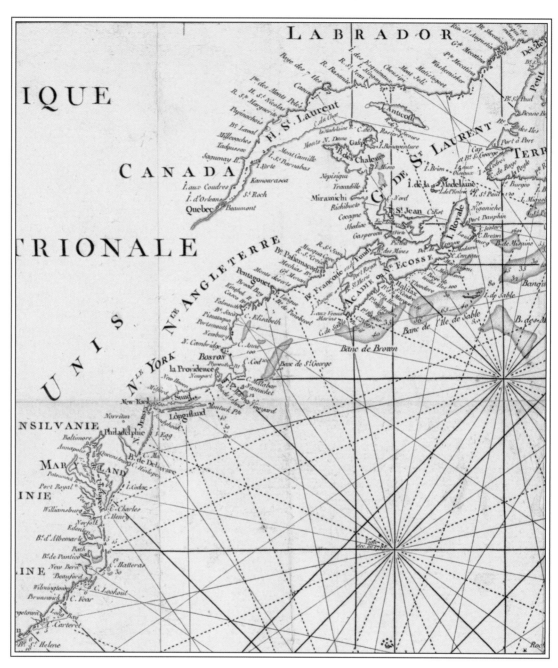

Detail from map on pages 32 and 33

Revolutionary Era

By the eve of the American Revolution, the farthest corners of Connecticut's approximately 5,000 square miles had been settled and organized into towns. Its population had increased dramatically, going from 130,000 in 1756 to 200,000 in 1774, almost entirely the result of a high birth rate. Some people were beginning to feel a bit cramped.

The people of Connecticut were still governing themselves under the liberal provisions of the Royal Charter of 1662. Connecticut was by now unique among the thirteen colonies in having the right to elect its own governor rather than having one appointed by the British monarch.

As the dispute between Great Britain and its colonies over taxation and the control it represented grew increasingly tense in the 1760s, the role of the Connecticut River as an economic, political, and cultural dividing line became increasingly obvious. The river cleaves the state roughly in half from north to south. In the colonial era it was a significant barrier to east-west travel. It could be traversed only by ferry; the first bridge to span it within Connecticut would not be built until the nineteenth century.

The eastern half of the colony, which traded more frequently with Puritan Boston, not surprisingly tended to share the Massachusetts patriots' attitude of resistance toward the British efforts to exert increasing control over the colonies via taxation. Thus the eastern portion of the colony was more radical, more likely to demonstrate defiance. For Puritans, opposition to British tyranny was entwined with their faith.

West of the river, particularly in the southwestern portion of the colony, the primary economic and cultural connections were with New York, a multicultural, more broad-minded, and more religiously diverse and tolerant society than that of Massachusetts. It was also a more prosperous region than the eastern portion of the colony. In addition, southwestern Connecticut was home to the colony's largest concentration of parishes of the Church of England, which acknowledged the British monarch as the church's earthly head. That fact made opposition to the crown's policies a particularly personal dilemma for Anglicans, as Church of England members were called.

As a consequence of these factors, fervor for opposing British policies was considerably less fierce than east of the river.

The British Parliament's passage in 1765 of the Stamp Act, intended to raise revenue by taxing paper goods, such as legal documents and newsprint, sold in the colonies, highlighted this east-west divide and altered the balance of power in Connecticut. Elections for governor were held annually in Connecticut. Once a man had been elected to that position, voters typically returned him to office year after year, until he died or stepped down voluntarily. The custom was one source of Connecticut's nickname of the "Land of Steady Habits."

Thomas Fitch of Norwalk on the southwestern coast had been governor for a dozen years when news of the Stamp Act's passage reached Connecticut. Although Fitch personally opposed the tax, he felt duty-bound as governor to swear to enforce it.

Radicals who opposed the Stamp Act, most of them from east of the Connecticut River, proceeded to upset the status quo of the colony's gubernatorial politics. They organized into groups known as the Sons of Liberty and, in 1766, nominated an opposing slate, including William Pitkin, who came from the section of Hartford east of the Connecticut River, for governor.

Pitkin was victorious and won reelection as governor every year until his death in 1769. He was succeeded by Jonathan Trumbull Sr. of Lebanon in eastern Connecticut, a solid supporter of resistance to British oppression.

When the American Revolution broke out in 1775, Jonathan Trumbull was the only colonial governor to side with the patriot cause. When the Declaration of Independence was adopted in 1776, Connecticut's governing body simply passed legislation deleting references to the King of England in its Royal Charter of 1662 and continued to govern itself under the provisions of that venerable document. Jonathan Trumbull Sr. was reelected as governor every year throughout the Revolution, and he supervised Connecticut's participation in the war for independence from his country store turned war office in Lebanon.

Connecticut's geographical position in New England enabled it to play a critical role in the war for independence. The state's interior was largely spared the ravages of troops tromping through on military campaigns, of actual battles, or of foraging parties sent out by foe and friend alike. Farmers thus isolated from the devastation of war were able to grow crops and raise livestock without disruption. Much of what those Connecticut farmers produced, including corn, rye, wheat, swine, and cattle, went to feed the soldiers of the Continental Army. One particularly dramatic episode demonstrated both Connecticut's role as a source of sustenance for hungry soldiers and Governor Trumbull's commitment to doing whatever was necessary to support the fight for independence. In the dead of winter, General George Washington sent out a desperate appeal from Valley Forge to feed his starving troops. Connecticut responded by driving a herd of cattle over frozen, snow-clogged roads.

Later in the war, Connecticut's location between New York, where General George Washington maintained his headquarters on the Hudson River, and Rhode Island, where a portion of the French troops sent by King Louis XVI to assist the Americans' fight for independence were stationed, would make it the scene of several pivotal developments in the war. French troops actually spent the winter of 1780–81 in Lebanon and surrounding towns, stationed there largely because they could find resources. When George Washington wanted to meet with the Comte de Rochambeau, stationed in Rhode Island, to discuss the strategy that would ultimately lead to the battle of Yorktown and victory for American independence, the logical choice was somewhere midway between the two military camps—the town of Wethersfield, Connecticut. Following that conference, French troops made a memorable march across Connecticut to rendezvous with the Continental Army for their joint effort.

For towns all along Connecticut's coastline, the American Revolution meant something drastically different. The British took control of New York, including Long Island, in late summer of 1776, and held them until the very end of the war in 1783.

In the period immediately following the capture of New York, the war meant divisions, dislocation, and devastation for many Connecticut residents who had made up their minds to remain loyal to the British crown. For many Anglicans, the split constituted a crisis of conscience. Hundreds of Connecticut Loyalists sought sanctuary behind the British lines in New York, abandonning homes and possessions that were subject to confisca-tion by the government. They also frequently left behind loved ones, as disagreement over which side to choose in what was essentially a civil war drove a wedge between family members, friends, and neighbors. During the same period, there was a reverse flow of Patriots from New York and Long Island seeking refuge in Connecticut.

For the rest of the war, only the waters of Long Island Sound separated Connecticut from enemy territory, often visible on the horizon. The shoreline was constantly exposed to surprise attack from the water. Nearly every town along the coast experienced harassment by the enemy, both British troops and Loyalists, ranging from raids and skirmishes undertaken by a handful of men to invasions by forces of hundreds of soldiers. British assaults led to the near-total destruction by fire of the towns of Fairfield, Norwalk, and New London, and to the deaths of many men who fought to defend their homeland, including more than 150 on a single day of carnage.

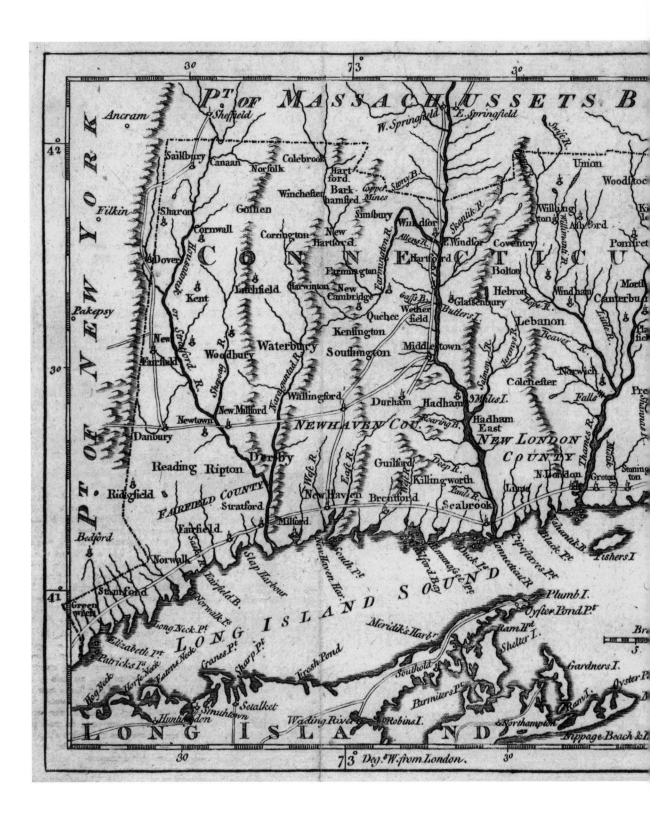

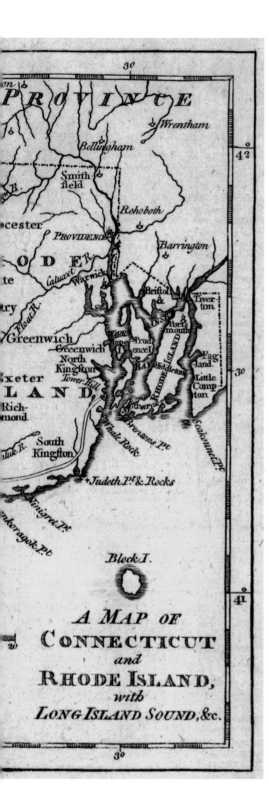

A map of Connecticut and Rhode Island with Long Island Sound, &c.—(1776)

By the end of 1776, the British controlled all of modern metropolitan New York and Long Island, which lurked as an ever-present threat. For the remainder of the war, seven long years, Connecticut's coastline would be in constant danger of raids launched from New York and Long Island.

Residents never knew if the day, or night, might bring an enemy attack, as forces large and small of British troops, Hessian mercenaries, and Loyalists regularly harassed Connecticut's shoreline towns. Fairfield, Norwalk, and New London were almost totally destroyed by fire during surprise attacks by enemy troops who arrived by ship. Other towns came under attack as well, including New Haven, Groton, Stonington, Guilford, and Madison.

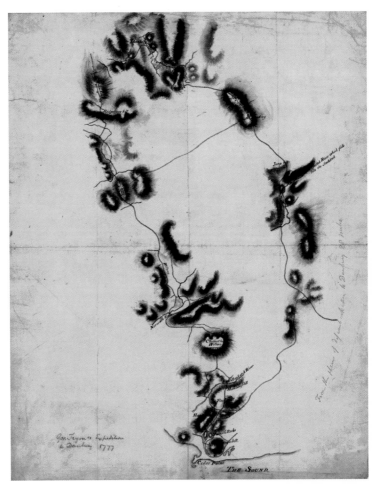

Gov. Tryon's expedition to Danbury—(1777)

The danger that proximity to British-controlled New York meant for Connecticut was made clear early in the American Revolution. On April 25, 1777, a force of approximately 1,800 British regulars and Loyalists from New York came ashore from two dozen ships on the beach at present-day Westport. Led by Major General William Tryon, who was also Royal Governor of New York, they marched approximately 28 miles north along the eastern side of the circular route depicted to their target, the patriots' cache of military supplies in Danbury.

The British set fire to the supplies and to more than a dozen buildings in Danbury. Having learned that patriot militiamen were assembling along the route the British had taken to reach Danbury, Tryon took a different way back to the waiting ships on Long Island Sound.

Near the town of Ridgefield, the retreating British encountered armed opposition from militia forces, who both engaged the enemy in combat and harassed them as they marched until, on April 28, they finally reached the coast and the safety of the transport vessels that had brought them from New York. Patriot losses were estimated at twenty dead and eighty wounded.

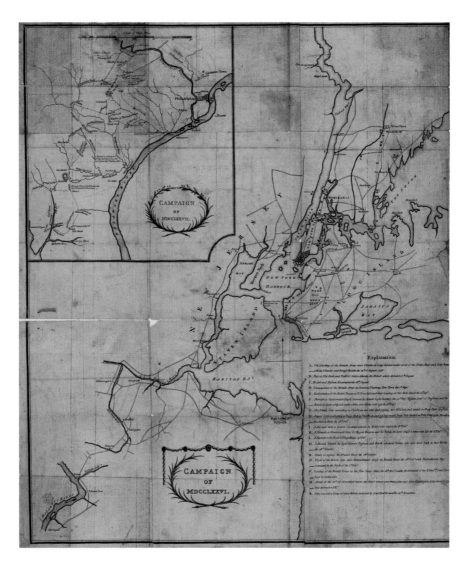

Campaign of MDCCLXXVI—(1780?)

Although Connecticut does not appear on this map, the events it depicts had major repercussions for the state and its residents. The cartographer chronicles the series of battles and skirmishes that occurred from August to November of 1776, in which British, Hessian, and Loyalist troops drove the Continental Army off Long Island, then Manhattan, then forced them to retreat far to the north until they were uncomfortably close to Connecticut. For the rest of the war, the British would take advantage of their proximity to Connecticut to launch raids large and small on its coastline.

Hundreds of Connecticut troops fought in the first engagement of this campaign, the disastrous Patriot defeat at the Battle of Long Island. Many were killed, wounded, or taken prisoner.

*Marche de l'armée française de Providence
à la Rivière du Nord—(1781)*

French troops sent to aid the American struggle for independence arrived in Rhode Island in 1780. The following summer, they marched west across Connecticut to rendezvous with the Continental Army under General George Washington at its headquarters on the "North" or Hudson River in New York.

French forces followed two different routes across Connecticut, depicted on these three maps. The Comte de Rochambeau, commander of all the French allied troops in America, followed the route that passed through Hartford. It took Rochambeau's troops thirteen days to cross Connecticut, during which they established nine camps. The second force of French, commanded by the Duc de Lauzun, followed a route south of Rochambeau's, through Middletown.

The original plan called for the combined French and American armies to attack British-held New York. But the arrival of the French fleet off the coast of Virginia caused the Franco-American force to continue its march past New York. The campaign concluded with the allied French and American armies and the French fleet defeating the British army, led by General Cornwallis, at Yorktown, Virginia, on October 19, 1781, a victory that secured American independence.

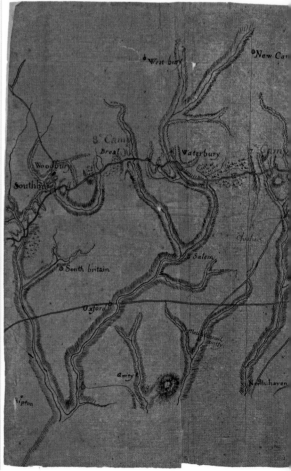

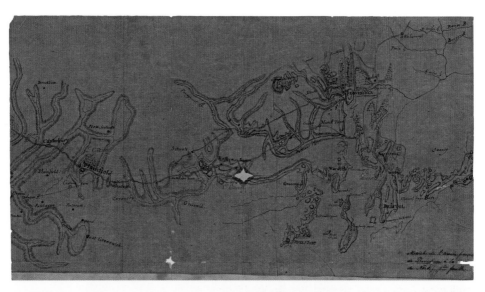

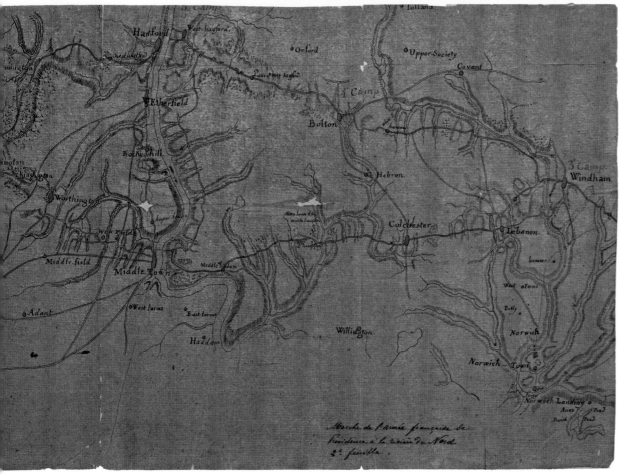

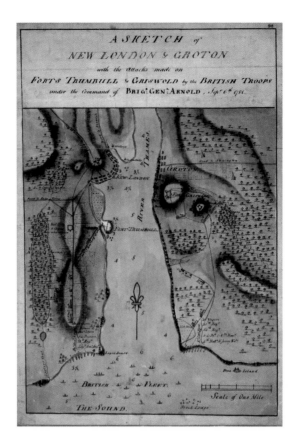

A sketch of New London & Groton with the attacks made on Forts Trumbull & Griswold by the British troops under the command of Brigr. Genl. Arnold, Sept. 6th. 1781—Lyman (1781)

This neatly drawn, precise map depicts events that unfolded when a combined invasion force of British regulars, Hessian mercenaries, and Loyalists landed on the Connecticut coast at the mouth of the Thames River on September 6, 1781. But the Loyalist artist neglected to illustrate the destruction and slaughter that resulted from these carefully rendered maneuvers.

The Thames had been home port to dozens of "privateers"—private vessels authorized by the state or federal government to seize enemy ships in a time of war. Privateers had inflicted serious damage on both British naval and civilian shipping, while the cargoes of captured vessels had helped ease the Continental Army's chronic shortage of supplies.

Destroying this "detestable nest of pirates" was the goal of the 1,700-man enemy force that had sailed from New York under the command of Benedict Arnold, who after betraying the Patriot cause had become an officer in the British army.

The invaders came ashore in two separate groups of approximately eight hundred each, which proceeded to march up both banks of the Thames River. On the New London side, Fort Trumbull fell easily, after which privateers that had not managed to escape farther up the river were set on fire, along with goods in warehouses on New London's wharves.

The flames quickly spread—unintentionally, according to the enemy—to other structures, and all but a few of New London's buildings burned to the ground. Across the river at Fort Griswold, far worse was about to unfold.

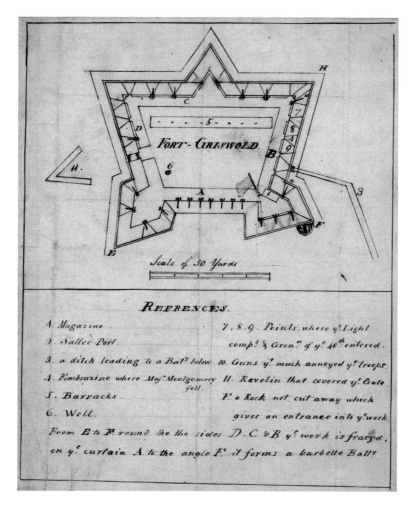

Fort-Griswold—(1781?)

By the time the invasion force reached Fort Griswold on the Groton side, 158 men and boys, most having hastily answered the alarm from surrounding towns, had gathered within its walls. The defenders proceeded to repeatedly repulse the better-equipped and -trained invaders, who outnumbered them five to one, using, among other weapons, the artillery that the British-sympathizing artist identified as the "guns yt much annoyed ye troops." Dozens of the invaders were wounded or killed, including British "Major Montgomery," the site of whose death is noted on the map.

Fort Griswold's commander, Colonel William Ledyard, refused a British demand to surrender the post, even after the enemy warned him that if they captured it, they would show "no quarter"—that is, no mercy for its defenders.

The garrison was unable to keep the enemy from overrunning Fort Griswold's poorly maintained defenses. The victors, perhaps enraged by the extraordinarily stubborn resistance they had encountered, proceeded to butcher the patriots. In less than an hour, more than eighty defenders of Fort Griswold, including Colonel Ledyard, were killed, some of them mangled beyond recognition. Dozens more were seriously injured in what came to be known as the "Massacre at Fort Griswold."

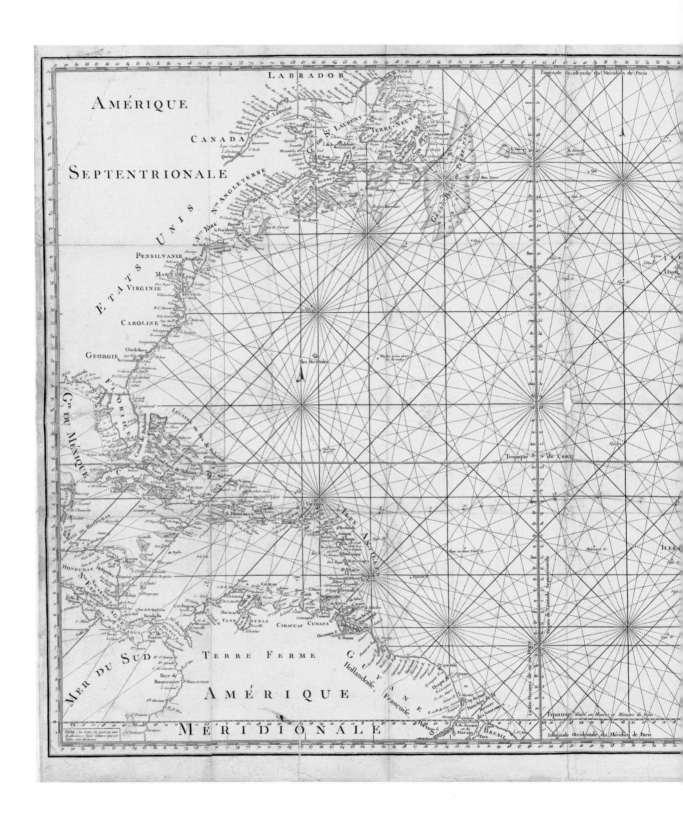

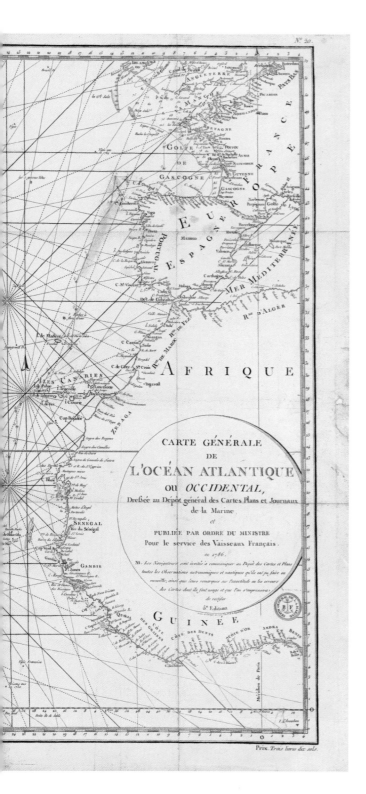

Carte générale de l'Océan Atlantique ou Occidental, dressée au Dépôt général des cartes, plans, et journaux de la marine, et publiée par ordre du Ministre pour le service des vaisseaux français en 1786

By the late 1700s, maritime trade had been established between Connecticut coastal and river ports such as New London, Middletown, and Hartford and the islands of the West Indies, including Barbados, Jamaica, and Grenada. Connecticut vessels also traded regularly at ports on the North American coast such as New York and Philadelphia. Connecticut's main export was the bounty of its farms, everything from beef to onions to wheat.

Among the items Connecticut imported from the West Indies were nutmegs—small, hard globes that were grated to produce powder to flavor all manner of foods. Yankee peddlers included nutmegs in the collection of goods they sold in all parts of the United States east of the Mississippi River. The peddlers, most of whom were from Connecticut, gained a reputation for driving a hard bargain—and for sometimes tricking their customers. The legend grew that peddlers sold wooden "nutmegs" instead of the genuine article to unsuspecting housewives. Hence the nickname of the "Nutmeg State."

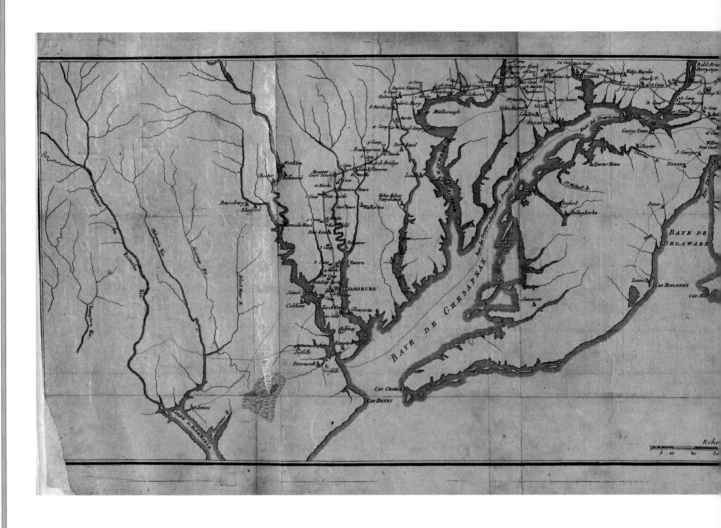

Differents camps de l'armée de York-town à Boston—Soulés (1787)

British General George Cornwallis's surrender of his army to the combined American and French forces at York-town, Virginia, on October 19, 1781, was a defeat so severe that it ultimately guaranteed the Patriots' victory in the war for independence. But it would take some time for that to become evident, and fighting continued.

The French forces who had marched through Connecticut in the summer of 1781 on their way to Yorktown

remained in Virginia for more than a year. They began the long trek back to Boston, from which they would sail for home, in June of 1782. They retraced much the same route as Rochambeau's troops had taken the previous year. This map includes the location of the camps in Connecticut on the journey from Providence to Yorktown, numbered 3 to 11, and from Yorktown to Boston, numbered 40 to 49.

Connecticut, from the best authorities—Doolittle (1795?)

Amos Doolittle's map of Connecticut at the end of the eighteenth century notes features both ancient and relatively new—at least by New England standards. "Dickswells Cave" in modern West Haven refers to the cave in which John Dixwell, one of the "regicides" who signed the death warrant of King Charles I of England in 1649, hid from royal pursuit. "Shachems Head" in Guilford is so-called because the head of a Pequot tribe sachem killed during the Pequot War in 1637 was displayed in the crotch of a tree at that place for many years.

"Newgate" refers to the copper mine in modern-day East Granby that Connecticut transformed into a prison in 1773. The "Shaking Quakers," printed slightly north of the town of Enfield, were an early community of the religious sect known as Shakers that was established there in 1780. The "Glassworks," in what today is the town of Manchester, launched a pioneering attempt in 1783 at manufacturing glass.

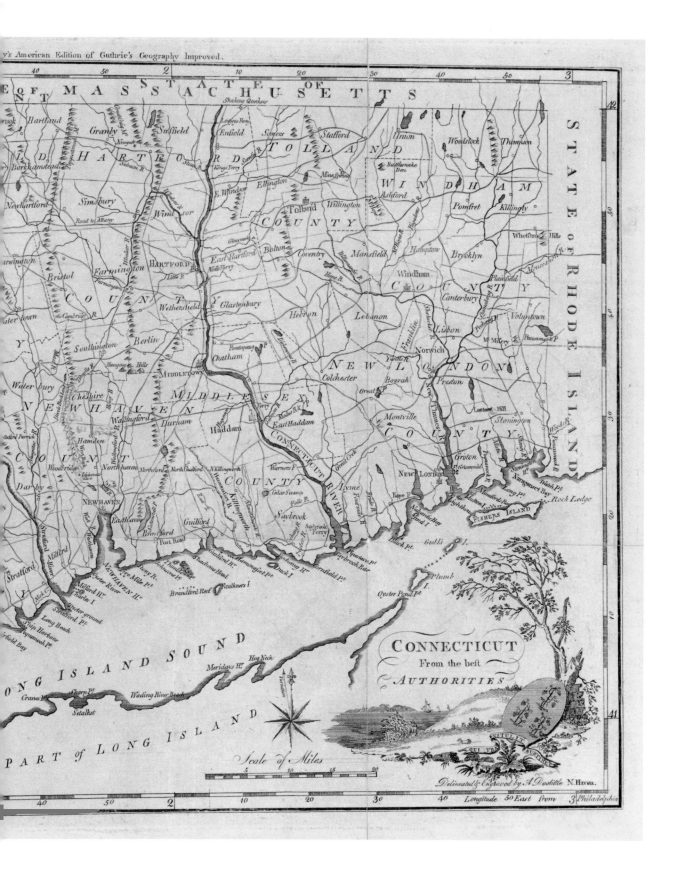

CONNECTICUT
From the best
AUTHORITIES

Delineated & Engraved by A. Doolittle N. Haven.

Scale of Miles

LONG ISLAND SOUND

PART of LONG ISLAND

Detail from map on pages 44 and 45

Nineteenth Century

BY THE FIRST QUARTER OF THE NINETEENTH century, Connecticut's economy was stagnant. All of the state's acreage had long been settled. Farmers divided their land holdings among their sons, who in turn divided their portion among their sons, so that after several generations few men received enough acres from their fathers to support a family. Scarcity had made land so expensive that purchasing additional acres was rarely an option. And much of it was worn out, its fertility depleted by 150 years of cultivation.

The coastal and West Indies trade that had provided an alternate livelihood to working the land had been severely damaged by the disruption of shipping during the War of 1812 and events leading up to it. Beyond farming and seafaring, there were few ways to make a living in Connecticut in the early 1800s.

People had been moving out of Connecticut even before the American Revolution, seeking fresh opportunity in the form of inexpensive land on the frontier. By the late 1700s, that flow of emigrants had turned into a torrent, as tens of thousands of people left their homes to get a new start in wilderness or near-wilderness areas such as Vermont, northeastern Pennsylvania, and

upstate New York. A particularly popular destination was the section of what today is northeastern Ohio, originally known as the Connecticut Reserve or the Western Reserve. Connecticut had laid claim to these acres based on the extension of its northern and southern boundaries to the "western sea" as spelled out in its Royal Charter of 1662. Although the land eventually was made part of Ohio, Connecticut was permitted to sell the acres to investors who in turn sold it to individuals. A portion of the Western Reserve was set aside to compensate victims of the British attacks on the Connecticut coast during the Revolution.

Thus while the young nation's population skyrocketed, Connecticut's only crept up. Many towns actually declined in population. By 1830, Connecticut also had the most homogeneous population of any state, with the vast majority of its residents being white Protestants of British ancestry. The people of African descent, who constituted less than 3 percent of the population, were the only significant minority group.

But in this slump many individuals who had remained in Connecticut were inspired to rethink the old ways of doing things. The land might have reached the limit of what it could offer in the way of farming, but it offered other features that entrepreneurs took advantage of to implement their new ideas.

Ingenious Connecticut residents devised new ways to produce all manner of goods faster, more efficiently, and for a lower cost. The development of interchangeable parts and the assembly line were essential elements in this fledgling industrial revolution. In many cases a key factor was also the harnessing of the force of swift-flowing rivers and streams with the potential to generate sufficient water power to operate the new factories.

Ingenious entrepreneurs combined their innovative ideas with the power of the state's dammed waterways to establish new industries. A few examples include Eli Terry making clocks in his factory in Plymouth; Eli Whitney and the firearms factory he set up on the Mill River in Hamden; and brothers Samuel and David Collins, who set up their ax factory on the Farmington River in Canton.

Steam power provided the next boost to Connecticut's rise as an industrial center. The railroad arrived in the state in 1839, and by the eve of the Civil War, train tracks crisscrossed the state, connecting population centers with each other and with other states. Railroads made it feasible and affordable to bring in raw materials for factories to transform into finished products that other trains would then carry away to be sold to markets around the world.

The development of steam engines to power machinery meant that factories were no longer tethered to the banks of a river or stream. New industries sprang up across the state to join the existing ones, which often continued to make use of their water power resources.

During the Civil War, Connecticut factories made a major contribution toward supplying Union soldiers with arms and ammunition, as well as uniforms, bayonets, buttons, and rubber footwear. Following the war, Connecticut industry grew at a phenomenal pace. The number of manufacturing firms in the state nearly doubled during a thirty-year period, from 5,128 in 1870 to more than 9,000 in 1900. Some towns specialized in certain products, like clocks in Plymouth, brass in Waterbury, and silver in Meriden. Others were home to a wide variety of factories.

The rise of industry changed the literal face of Connecticut. The new factories required thousands of workers to operate the equipment and man the assembly lines. Immigrants from all over Europe began streaming into Connecticut to take jobs making hardware, rubber goods, silk fabric, firearms, cotton thread, typewriters, bicycles, automobiles, silver, household appliances, and countless more products.

By 1870 one out of every four Connecticut residents had been born in a foreign country—a radical change from the status quo just four decades earlier. A significant number of newcomers, especially the Irish, were members of the Roman Catholic Church, which Connecticut's Puritan founders had considered little better than idolatry. The steeples of Catholic churches began to join those of Protestant denominations in communities with significant immigrant populations.

At the turn of the twentieth century, Connecticut had been transformed. In 1830 it had been a land of small towns connected only by water or rough roads and turnpikes, with an agriculture-based economy and a population composed overwhelmingly of individuals who shared an ethnic heritage, religion, and culture that had dominated for nearly two centuries. In 1900 it was a manufacturing powerhouse, dotted with burgeoning cities, crisscrossed by train tracks, with a polyglot, multicultural, multifaith population that was growing ever larger and more diverse. It was a juggernaut that would continue into the next century.

Thanks to the convenience of train travel, Connecticut also now had a single capital city. Since any location in the state was within a couple hours' train ride of any other, New Haven was demoted, and Hartford became the sole capital in 1875.

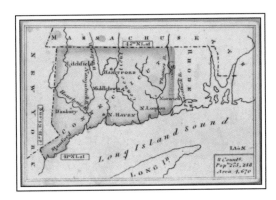

Geographical conversation cards: states of the United States—Melish (1824)

The flash cards of their day, these "geographical conversation cards" featured a map of each state on one side and a few basic facts about it on the other. The Connecticut map marks both Hartford and New Haven as a capital city with a crude little building and includes the clarifying statement, "There are two seats of government, as in Rhode Island."

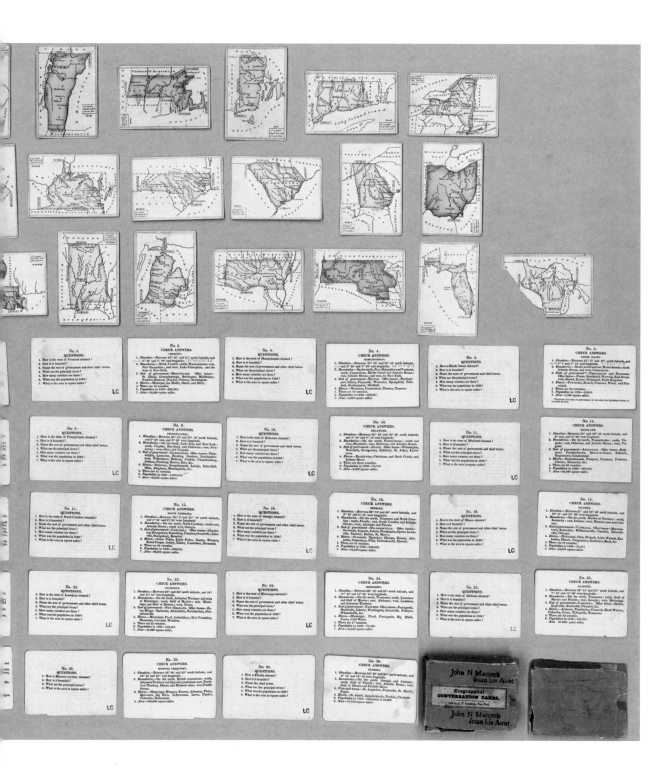

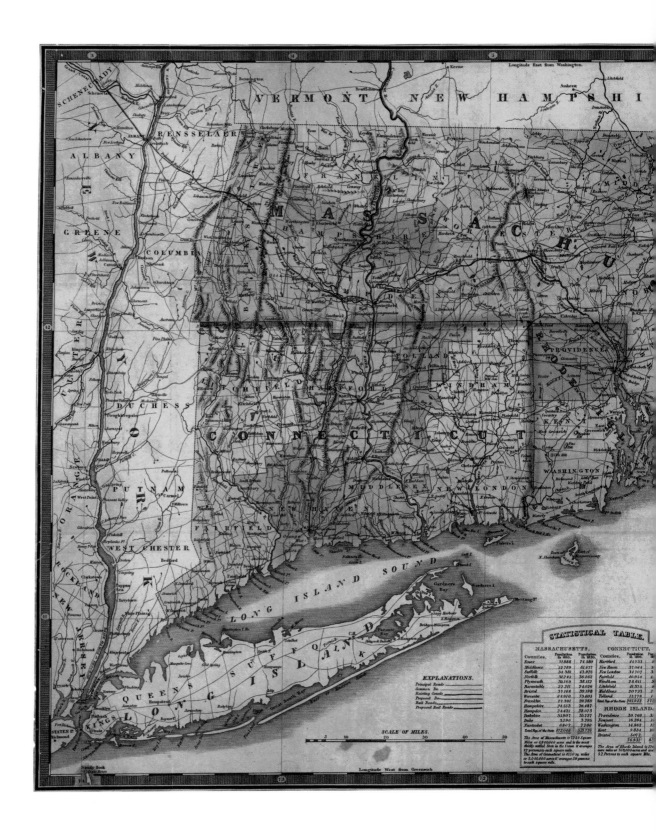

Map of Massachusetts, Connecticut, and Rhode Island;
constructed from the latest authorities—Young (1831)
During the first decades of the nineteenth century, new towns were being created from old towns in Connecticut so quickly that mapmakers had a hard time keeping up. This 1831 map claimed to have been based on "the latest authorities," but it does not show several of the nine towns that were created between 1819 and 1830. Connecticut's population density was reported at 59 people per square mile, which makes the state seem almost deserted when compared with the modern figure of more than 700 people per square mile.

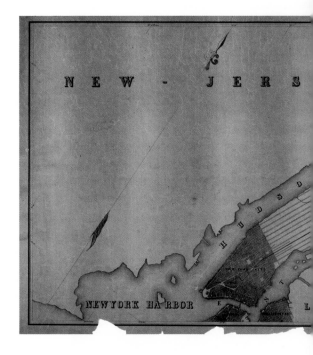

*Map exhibiting the experimental and located lines
for the New-York and New-Haven Rail-Road—
Anderson (1845)*

A dozen years after the first few miles of rail line opened in Connecticut, it was possible to take a train from New York to New Haven along the railway named for those two cities. Completion of the New York and New Haven Railroad in 1849 actually had an even greater significance, for it was the final link in a chain of rail lines that enabled a traveler to take the train from New York to Boston.

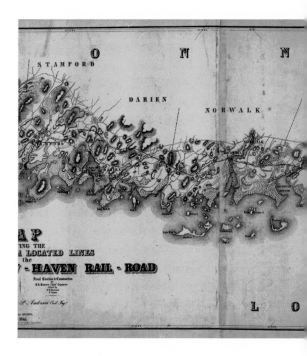

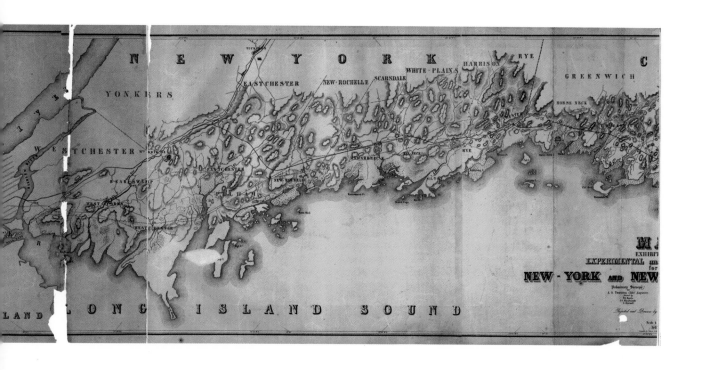

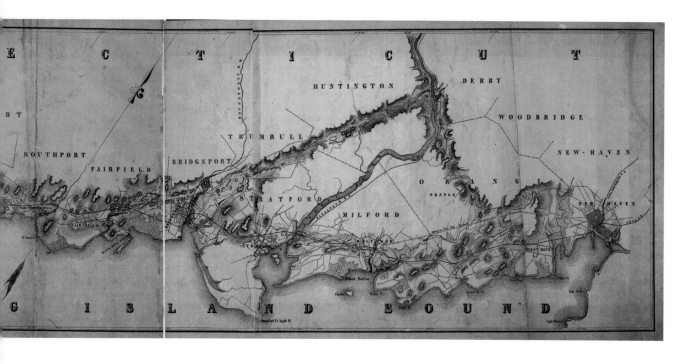

47

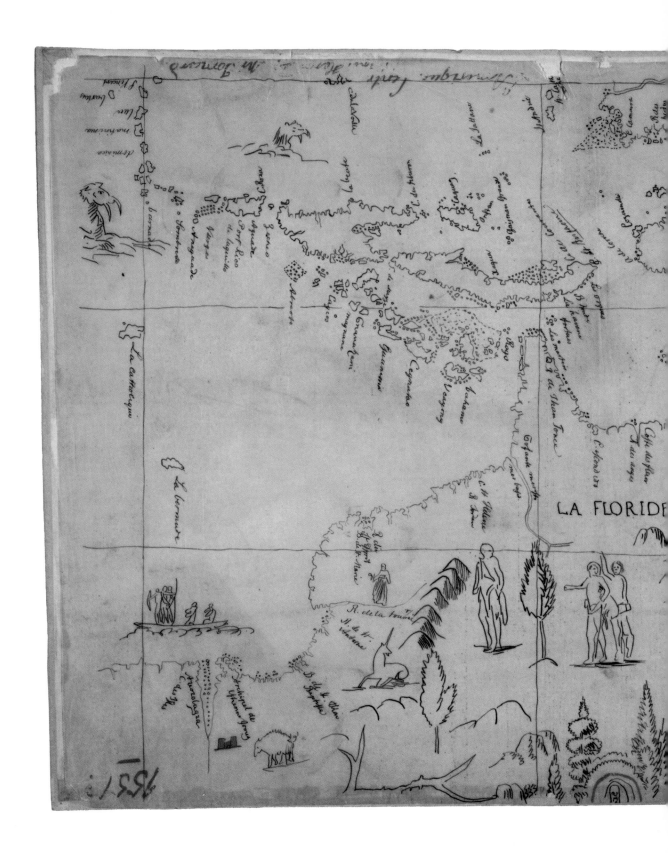

*L'Amérique centr[ale]; 1 jou [?],
Henri II—Jomard (ca. 1850)*

From the modern point of view, the New World is depicted upside down—that is, south is at the top—in this map of North America drawn in 1542 for King Henry II of France and published as part of a collection in the mid-1800s. New England, including Connecticut, can be located roughly in the lower left corner. In contrast to other areas of the map, it is depicted as a little-known region populated by Native Americans and strange animals that included, apparently, a unicorn.

Telegraph and Rail Road map of the New England States—Williams (1854)

By 1854 more than half a dozen rail lines crisscrossed Connecticut. They brought a surge of activity to existing economic centers like Hartford, New Haven, and New London. There was no easier way for their manufacturers to receive shipments of raw materials for factories, ship out finished products, and bring in workers.

Small towns that for nearly two centuries had been largely self-contained social and economic islands were suddenly connected to the world at large, a development that would radically change life for many residents.

Not everyone welcomed the iron horse. Residents of Suffield waged a successful campaign in 1843 to keep train tracks from being laid through their town.

Smith's map of Hartford County, Connecticut—Woodford (1855)

This big, colorful wall map of Hartford County almost overflows with information and imagery. Vignettes of the homes of prominent residents are interspersed with romanticized illustrations of the farming life that was disappearing even as it was being celebrated: swine, goats, horses, tools, a beehive, haying and shoeing horses and hunting rabbits. Surprising anachronistic images include a man fighting a bear and an Indian brave.

The vignettes also point out institutions of civic prominence and pride, including the Normal School in New Britain, a teacher training institution that today is Central Connecticut State University; the Connecticut Literary Institute in Suffield, known today as the Suffield Academy; and the State House in Hartford, today's Old State House museum.

Clark's map of Litchfield County, Connecticut—Hopkins (1859)

The high, steep-sided hills that kept portions of Litchfield County forested and lightly settled into the second half of the nineteenth century are illustrated on this map. The massive amount of detail on roads, structures, residents, mills, businesses, and factories allowed people to see where they lived like never before.

Map showing the line of the Connecticut
& Western Railroad and its connections—
G. W. & C. B. Colton & Co. (1871)

The Connecticut Western Railroad started at Hartford and meandered through northwestern Connecticut, running through Bloomfield, Tariffville, Simsbury, Collinsville, New Hartford, Winsted, Norfolk, Canaan, Salisbury, and Lakeville before reaching the New York border. One of the primary purposes of the railroad, completed in 1871, was to connect with other railroads to create a route to bring coal from Pennsylvania mines to Connecticut.

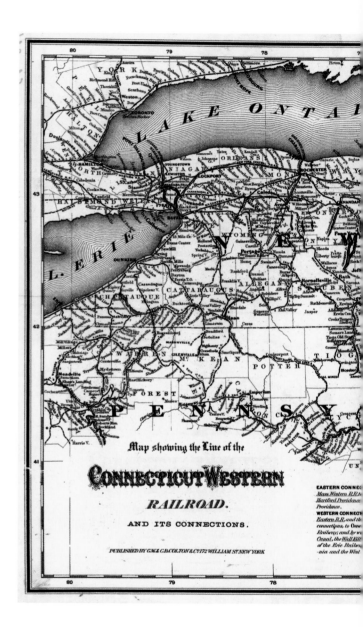

REFERENCE.

Connecticut Western Railroad .... colored Red

Rondout & Eastern R.R.and Connections " Blue

Dutchess & Columbia R.R.and Connections " Yellow

Massachusetts Western R.R. " Green

Hartford, Providence & Fishkill R.R.and Connections " Brown

SCALE of STATUTE MILES.

VIEW OF
NEW BRITAIN, CONN.
1875.

View of New Britain, Conn.—C. H. Vogt lith.
J. Knauber & Co. Print. (1875)
New Britain was well on the way to earning its title of Hardware Capital of the World when this view was published in 1875. It was home to two major hardware manufacturing firms, Russell & Erwin and Landers, Frary, and Clark, shown in the insets, and the seeds of a third had sprouted and would become the Stanley Works. The town's population had quadrupled in the quarter century since it had been set off as a separate municipality in 1850.

View of Bridgeport, Ct.—O. H. Bailey & Co. (1875)

Bridgeport in 1875 was becoming a major manufacturing center. Already its factories were turning out sewing machines, shirts, firearms, furniture, iron, steel, and much more.

Bridgeport in 1875 also had something no other city could claim— P. T. Barnum as its mayor. The world-famous showman, circus owner, and hoaxster, born in nearby Bethel, Connecticut, had lived in the city since 1846. His home, Waldemere, depicted in a vignette at the bottom of the view, was the third of four residences he occupied in the city. However outlandish an entrepreneur of entertainment Barnum might have been, he was entirely serious about improving his adopted city during his one-year stint as mayor and for years afterward, until his death in Bridgeport in 1891.

VIEW OF
1875.
BRIDGEPORT,
CT.

WHEELER & WILSON SEWING MACHINE WORKS.

"WALDEMERE" RESIDENCE OF P.T. BARNUM, ESQ.

PUBLIC BUILDINGS:

MANUFACTORIES:

BIRMINGHAM, CONN.
1876.

Birmingham, Conn.—O. H. Bailey & Co. (1876)

The section of the town of Derby between the Housatonic and Naugatuck Rivers became the borough of Birmingham in 1851. Its name paid homage to the industrial city in England that was home to so many manufacturing enterprises, particularly metal working, that it was famous as the Workshop of the World.

Connecticut's Birmingham boasted its own assortment of similar factories when this bird's-eye view was published in 1876, including the Birmingham Iron Foundry, which produced bayonets and gun barrels during the Civil War; the Norway Iron Bolt Works; the Birmingham Iron and Steel Works; the Derby Silver Company; and the Star Pin Manufactory. Birmingham ceased to exist as a borough, and its name began to fade from common use, when Derby was incorporated as a city in 1894.

View of Rockville, Conn.—
J. Knauber & Co. (1877)

The fact that Rockville's name was derived in the early 1800s literally from the fact of its rocky landscape might have seemed a less-than-optimistic omen for its future. But the village in the town of Vernon became so well known as a producer of woolen textiles that it was for a time called the Loom City. Several of the factories responsible for that renown are prominently featured in vignettes along the bottom of this view.

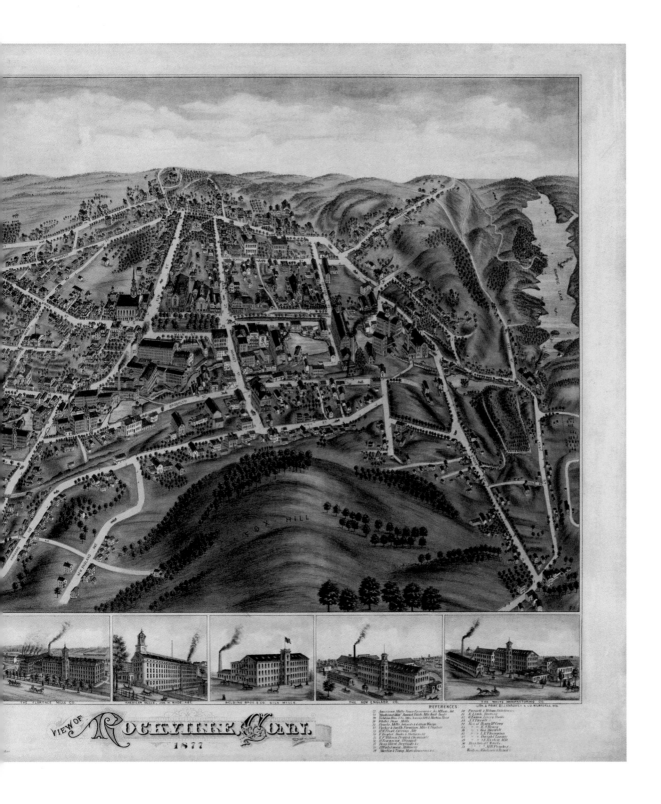

VIEW OF ROCKVILLE, CONN.
1877

O.H.BAILEY & CO. PUBLISHERS, BOSTON.

REFERENCES:

1 U S Post Office	*7 Congregational Church*
2 R R Depot	*8 Methodist "*
3 Charter Oak House	*9 Episcopal "*
4 Burnaps Block	*10 Romish "*
5 Mathers	*11 Graded School*
6 Coogan's "	*12 Seymour Paper Co*

VIEW OF WINDSOR LOCKS, CONN.
1877

REFERENCES:

13 A.W.Converse & Co.Foundry
14 E.Horton & Son Co.Patent Lathe Chucks
15 A.Dunham & Son Wool Cooling & Washing Works
16 Medlicott Co.Knit Goods
17 C.H.Dexter & Sons.Manilla Paper Mfct's.
18 " " " " Flour Grain & Saw Mill
19 J.H.Hayden & Son, Sewing Silk Mfct's.
20 Canal Paper Co.
21 Forest & Windsor Steel Works
22 J.P.Montgomery & Co Cotton Warps
23 Chas.W.Holbrook School Apparatus
24 T.Pease & Sons Co.Lumber,Sash,Blinds &c.

LITH.& PRINT.BY J.KNAUBER & CO.MILWAUKEE.WIS.

View of Windsor Locks, Conn.—
J. Knauber & Co. (1877)

The shallow stretch of rapids in the Connecticut River known as Enfield Falls stymied sailors for more than two centuries after Adriaen Block first encountered them in 1614. They ceased to be an obstacle to navigation with the 1829 completion of a five-mile canal with a lock that circumvented them. While the canal's service as a pathway was largely superseded by the railroad constructed in 1844, factories were established to take advantage of the water power it provided; all of this contributed to creating a substantial community along the canal. This bird's-eye view shows more than half a dozen factories producing a variety of goods, including paper and textiles, with shipping facilitated by the railroad. In 1854 a separate town that included the stretch of river along the locks was carved out and named Windsor Locks.

View of Stafford Springs, Conn.—O. H. Bailey & Co. (1878)

Stafford Springs took its name from the local mineral springs whose waters were believed to possess such healing qualities that people starting flocking to them as early as the 1700s. To accommodate those seeking relief by drinking or bathing in the water, a hotel operated in the early 1800s. It and the springs were purchased by the Honorable Julius Converse in 1886. By the end of the nineteenth century, the water was being bottled.

Stafford Springs became a borough of the town of Stafford in 1873, just a few years before this view was published. By that time a number of textile factories had been established.

VIEW OF,
STAFFORD SPRINGS, CONN.
1876.
PUBLISHED BY G.H.BAILEY & CO.BOSTON.

STAFFORD NATIONAL BANK.   CONVERSVILLE CO'S. MILLS.   RESIDENCE OF B.WELLS PATTEN.   RESIDENCE OF ROBBINS PATTEN.   GRANITE MILL CO.

REFERENCES.

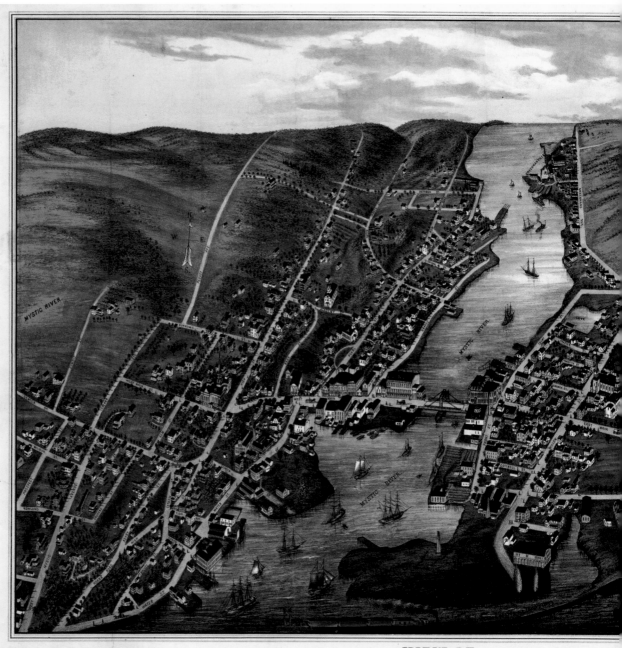

A. *St. Mark's Episcopal Church.*
B. *Union Baptist* do
C. *Congregational* do
D. *Methodist Episcopal* do
E. *St. Patrick's R Catholic* do
F. *Seventh Day Baptist* do
G. *Mystic River National Bank*
H. *First National Bank of Mystic Bridge.*
I. *Post Office*

VIEW OF
MYSTIC RIVER & MYSTIC BRIDGE, C
1879.
DRAWN & PUB. BY, O.H. BAILEY & J.C. HAZEN, BOSTON.

View of Mystic River & Mystic Bridge, Conn.—
O. H. Bailey & J. C. Hazen (1879)

There is no town of Mystic in Connecticut. The village of Mystic River on the western bank of the Mystic River is part of the town of Groton, while the village of Mystic Bridge on the eastern bank is included in the town of Stonington.

Shipbuilding had been a major industry for the Mystic region for much of the nineteenth century. Shipyards constructed all manner of vessels, including clipper ships, yachts, and steamboats. But that era was ending just as this bird's-eye view was published.

Other industries that had been established during the shipbuilding boom would help fill the employment gap. They included the Greenmanville Manufacturing Company, a producer of textiles.

View of Clinton, Connecticut—O. H. Bailey & Co. (1881)

The shoreline town of Clinton was among the communities that did not experience the industrialization, immigration, and urbanization that transformed much of Connecticut in the nineteenth century. However, Clinton did feel the impact of another economic development that was gaining momentum in the late 1800s: the emergence of Connecticut shoreline towns as vacation destinations for urbanites seeking temporary relief from the crowding, noise, pollution, grit, and hectic pace of the city. Hotels catering to vacationers went up in many towns along the coast, including Clinton's Bacon House, which proclaimed itself the "most popular summer resort on the Sound."

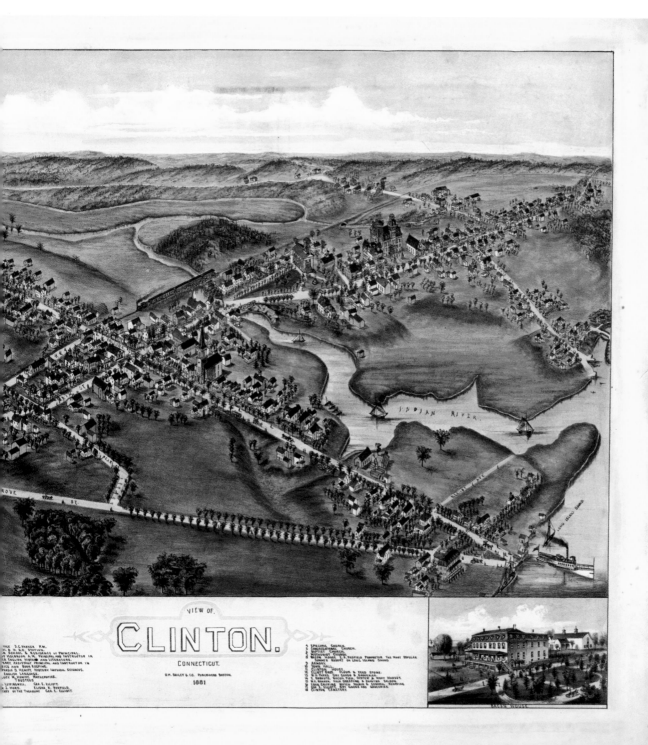

VIEW OF.

CLINTON.

CONNECTICUT.

O.H. BAILEY & CO. PUBLISHERS BOSTON.

1881

INDIAN RIVER.

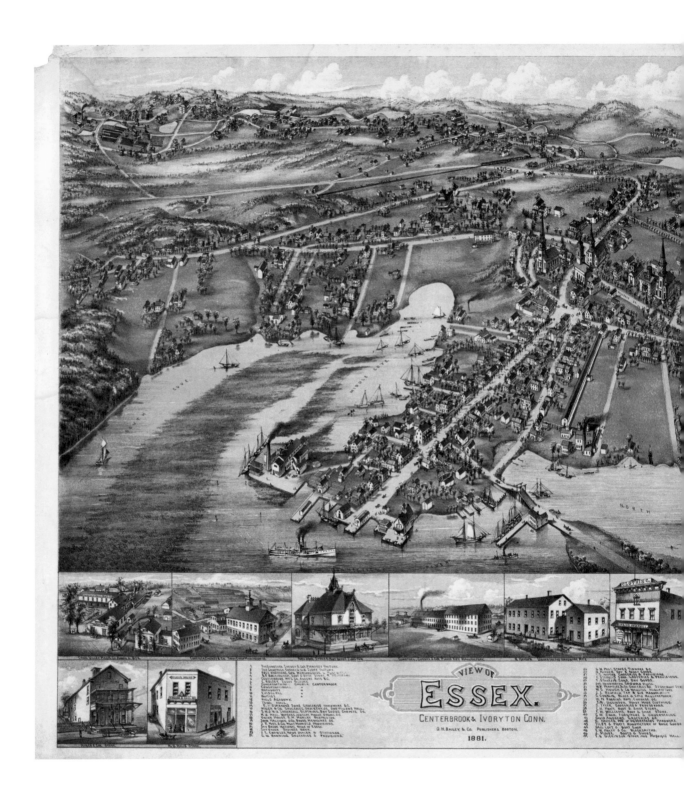

VIEW OF ESSEX.

CENTERBROOK & IVORYTON CONN.

O. H. BAILEY & Co. Publishers, Boston.

1881.

View of Essex, Centerbrook & Ivoryton, Conn.—O. H. Bailey & Co. (1881)

Essex is a prime example of a Connecticut town that has managed to retain much of its historic fabric and atmosphere. Many of the buildings shown on Main Street leading down the Connecticut River in this 1881 view still stand, from the 1852 Congregational Church (now minus its steeple, which was dismantled when it was discovered to have been poorly built and was never replaced) at its head to the W.H. Parmelee grocery store at the steamboat dock that today is home to the Connecticut River Museum.

The economic engine of Essex from the mid-1800s well into the twentieth century was Comstock, Cheney & Company. Located on the far western horizon (upper left corner) in this view, and also depicted in a vignette, the company made keys for pianos out of massive ivory elephant tusks imported from Africa. The increasing popularity in the nineteenth century of having a piano in one's home created a tremendous demand for what ordinarily might have seemed to be a highly specialized product. The community that grew up around the Comstock, Cheney & Company facility became known, quite logically, as Ivoryton.

View of Cheshire, Connecticut—O. H. Bailey & Co. (1882)
Buttons of all types were the trademark product of the town of Cheshire in the 1800s. The two major manufacturers, featured in vignettes on this 1882 bird's-eye view, were the Cheshire Manufacturing Company, founded in 1850, and the Cheshire Brass Company, established in 1866.

The Episcopal Academy, depicted at bottom center, was the pride of Cheshire nearly ninety years after its establishment in 1794. While the button factories have gone out of business, the Episcopal Academy continues to operate as the Cheshire Academy.

ACADEMY OF CONNECTICUT.   WALLACE HOUSE.   CHESHIRE MANUFACTURING COMPANY.   CHESHIRE BRASS COMPANY.

VIEW OF

CHESHIRE.

CONNECTICUT.

O. H. BAILEY & CO., PUB., BOSTON.

1882.

H. EPISCOPAL CHURCH.
I. CONGREGATIONAL CHURCH.
K. METHODIST CHURCH.
M. CATHOLIC CHURCH.
N. WALLACE HOUSE.
O. PAYNE'S HOTEL.
R. CHESHIRE MANUFACTURING CO.
S. PECK, STOWE & WILCOX CO.
T. BUTTON MANUFACTORY.
U. THE ACADEMY, STORE. C. A. STEELE PROPR.
V. M. M. CHAMBERLIN, M. D.
W. M. C. DOOLITTLE, MERCHANT TAILOR.
X. E. E. BROWN, GENERAL MDSE.
Z. GENERAL STORES.

75

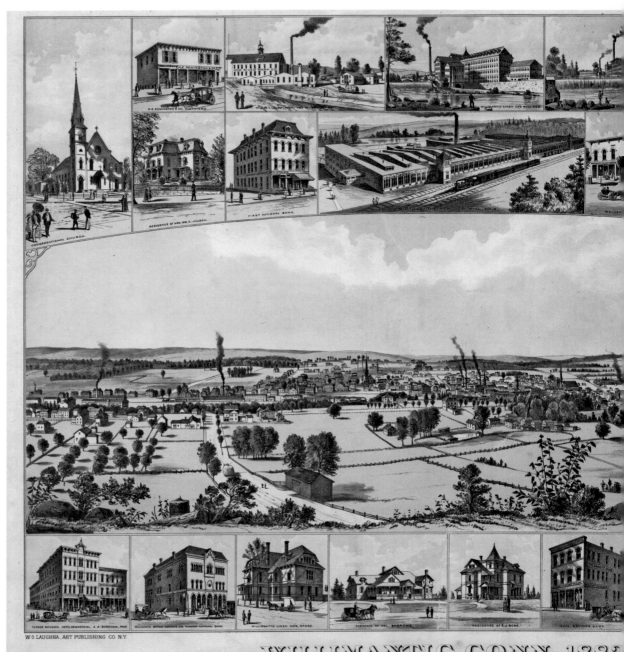

WILLIMANTIC, CONN., 1882

W.O. LAUGHNA, ART PUBLISHING CO. N.Y.

Willimantic, Conn.: From Blake Mountain—
Porter del., Hart Lith. (1882)

By 1882 Willimantic was well on the way to earning its nickname of the Thread City. The Willimantic Linen Company, founded in 1854, built a series of massive factories powered by the Willimantic River that became one of the largest thread manufacturers in the country. The company converted to making cotton thread in 1872, but kept its original name for more than two decades.

In 1898 the American Thread Company acquired the Willimantic Linen Company. American Thread ended production in Willimantic in 1985, but several of the factory buildings remain. Mill No. 2, shown at the top, built in 1864, survives as a handsome granite structure.

Stamford, Conn.—Burleigh (1883)

Fifty years earlier, Stamford had been a village of about 3,500 people. The arrival of the railroad not long afterward and construction of a canal that allowed vessels to navigate closer to the center of town made it an attractive location for manufacturing. By 1883 Stamford was home to dozens of factories that produced everything from carriages to billiard tables to wallpaper.

The city's major employer was the Yale & Towne Manufacturing Company, established in 1868 to make new and improved types of locks. The firm was so successful that it earned Stamford the nickname of the Lock City. Although Yale & Towne ended its Stamford operations in 1959, the company's significance in the community's history is still symbolized by two crossed Yale & Towne keys on the city seal.

Stamford, Conn.

13   Universalist Church.
20   St. John's Episcopal Church.
21   St. Andrew's Episcopal Church.
22   Meth-dist Episcopal Church.
23   Congregational Church.
24   Roman Catholic Church.
25   Meth-dist Chapel.
17   Y. M. C. A. Library.

28   Ferguson Library.
29   Public Schools.
30   First National Bank.
31   Stamford National Bank.
32   Stamford Savings Bank.
33   Stamford House.
33   Union House.
34   "The Arlington."
35   Hamilton House.

DRAWN & PUBLISHED BY GEO. E. NORRIS, BROCKTON, MASS. 1889.

COPYRIGHT SECURED.

1   J.H.Sessions & Son, Mf'rs Truck Hardware.
2   Sessions Foundry Co., Iron Founders.
3   The E.Ingraham Co., Clock Mfrs.
4   The Bristol Brass & Clock Co., { Bolting Mill.
                                    { Spoon Shop.
                                    { Lamp Burner Shop, Forrestville.
5   Bristol Mf'g Co., Mf'rs Knit Underwear.
6   N.S.Birge & Son,   "   "   "
7   The Case Wheel & Mill Co., S.W.Bradley, Treas. & M'g'r
        Grain Mills,National Water Wheel.
8   Dunbar Bros., Spring Mf'rs.
9   Wallace Barnes   "   Mf'r.
10 H.W.Barnes, Clock, Bells & Novelties.
11 S.E.Root, Clock Trimmings.
12 H.C.Thompson, Clock Mf'r.
13 The Horton Mf'g Co., Steel Fishing Rods.
14 C.A.Treadwell & Co. Machinists, Patterns, Dies,
        Punches Etc.
15 Everett Horton, Steel Pinions, Clock & Special Machinery
16 C.J.Root, Brass Butts and Toys.
17 Bristol Saw Works, E.O.Penfield.
18 W.Giddings & Son, Carriage M'frs.
19 F.Brainard, Hardware Specialties.
20 Geo.W.Eddy, Spring Mf'r.
21 A.P.Williams, Incubator Mf'r.
22 H.J.Mills, Paper Box Mf'r.
23 Clayton Bros, General Hardware Mf'rs.
24 Frank Clayton & Co., Carriage Washers.
25 L.Goodenough, Brass Foundry.
26 S.G.Monce, Mf'r of Glass Cutters Etc.
27 Frank Downs, Grist & Feed Mill.
27 Waite & Porter, Tin, Copper & Sheet Iron Ware Mf'rs.
28 Geo.C.Arms, Marble and Granite Works.
29 Geo.M.Eaton, Grain Elevator and Steam Mills.
30 S.P.Thompson & Son, Carriage Wheels Etc.
31 J.R.Mitchell & Son, Dry Goods, Clothing, Hats, Caps,
        and Furnishing Goods.
33 A.J.Muzzy, Dry Goods, Carpets, Millinery, Wall Paper &c
34 Sigourney Bros., Wholesale Fruit and Produce.
34 H.S.Goodale, Stoves, Ranges and Furnaces.
35 J.W.Skelly & Son, Hardware, Plumbing, Steam Fitting
        and Tin.
36 S.A.Olcott, Stoves, Ranges and Furnaces, Tin, Copper
        and Granite Ware.
36 Geo.D.Stewart, Painters' Supplies.
37 P.J.Coleman, Regular Plumber and Steam Fitter,
        Depot for Pipe, Steam and Water Supplies.
38 S.A.Weldon & Son, Hardware and Paints.
39 W.B.Woodruff, Groceries and Crockery.
40 C.A.Lane, Fancy Groceries and Crockery.
41 Webster & Ives, Groceries and Crockery.
41 Chas.A.Garrett, General Groceries.
42 Merriman Bros., Druggists.
43 Strong & Clark, Meat and Vegetables.
43 C.B.Ives & Co., Meat and Vegetables.
34 M.L.Gaylord, North Side Market.

BRISTOL, CONN.
LOOKING NORTH-EAST.

THE BURLEIGH LITH. EST., TROY, N.Y.

Bristol, Conn. looking northeast—
Norris (1889)
Bristol was home to many of the Connecticut manufacturers that turned out millions of clocks in the nineteenth century. The output of these factories was so massive that at one time Connecticut was known as the Clock State.

Riggs & Co., { C.H.Riggs. } { "Shoe Store" }
{ A.B.Eastwood. } { Boots & Shoes. }
an Bros., Boots and Shoes.
d & Mader, Clothing and Hats.
..berts, Jewelry and Crockery.
..bley, Furniture and Undertaking.
..Drescher, Harness & House Clothing M'f'r & Dealer
..Sirtess, Bakery and Confectionery.
.. Coal and Wood Yard.
'T.Cook, Bakery and Confectionery.
.Levitt, Trucking & General Freight Forwarding.
Ward, Hack, Livery & Express Stable.
McMellen, Livery, Hack & Boarding Stables.
..ott & Whelan, Livery, Hack, Boarding & General
Trucking Stables & Coal Dealers.
.Morse, Livery, Feed & Boarding Stables.
.Saxton, Lumber Dealer & Masons' Supplies.
..ers Bros., Contractors & Builders.
.Woodin, Agt., Contractor & Builder.

37 F.H.Williams, M.D. Office 141 Main St.
38 W.W.Horton, M.D.   "   117   "
39 H.E.Way, M.D.,   "   203   "
48 Dr. L.W.Robinson, Dentist.
50 Pierce & Winslow, Attorneys at Law.
59 H.N.Gale, Photographer.
60 Chas.H.Bunnell, Turner of Foriegn and Domestic Woods.
     Small Tool Handles a Specialty.
61 Welch's Clock Case Shop.
62 G.W.Neubauer, Wood Turning & Carving.
63 Marbleized Clock Case Mfy.
A   Bristol National Bank.
     Treadway & Stevens, Fire, Life & Accident Insurance.
     John J.Jennings, Attorney at Law.
B   C.V.Mason, Insurance & Real Estate,Gridley Block.
C   Savings Bank & Town Offices.
D   Commercial House, C.F.Michael.
E   Bristol House, Chas.H.Tiffany.

F   Gridley House.
G   Michael's Opera House.
H   Town Hall.
I   Post Office.
R   Bristol Herald.
J   Bristol Press.
K   Schools.
L   R.R.Station.
M   Electric Lighting Station.
N   Copper Mine.
O   Forestville.
P   Polkville.
Q   Brightwood, A.F.Atkins.
R   Highlawn, S.W.Bradley.
S   J.H.Sessions, Residence.
T   J.H.Sessions, Jr.
U   W.E.Sessions,   "
V   Wallace Barnes, "

W   W.H.Nettleton, Residence.
X   Truman F.Judd,   "
Y   C.S.Treadway,   "
Z   F.Q.Hayward,   "
a   E.N.Hollister,   "
b   J.F.Cose,   "
c   A.Curtis,   "
d   Fred Davey,   "
e   Congregational Church.
f   Methodist Church.
g   Baptist Church.
h   Episcopal Church.
i   St.Joseph's Catholic Church.
j   Advent Christian Church.
48 Y.M.C.A.

Terryville, Ct., Litchfield Co.—
Norris (1894?)

Although actually part of the town of Plymouth, Terryville was well known in its own right
in the nineteenth century as a center of lock
manufacturing. Eli Terry Jr. used the force of
the Pequabuck River to operate the Eagle Manufacturing Company in 1854. The company,
shown left of center in this 1894 bird's-eye
view, flourished for more than a century, shipping locks around the globe, and the section of
town in which it was located came to be known
as Terryville after the company's founder.

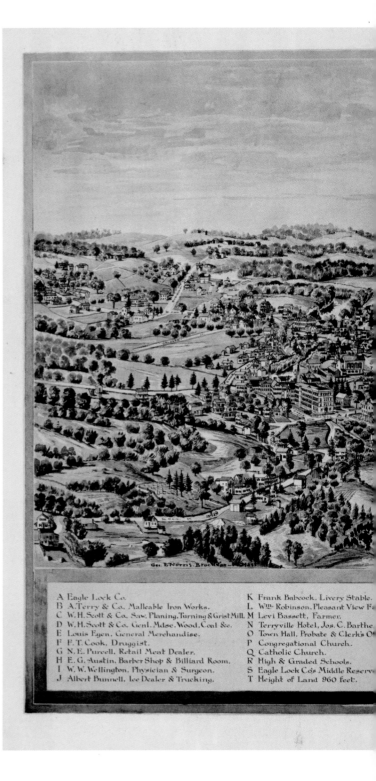

A Eagle Lock Co.
B A. Terry & Co. Malleable Iron Works.
C W. H. Scott & Co. Saw, Planing, Turning & Grist Mill.
D W. H. Scott & Co. Genl. Mdse. Wood, Coal &c.
E Louis Egen, General Merchandise.
F F. T. Cook, Druggist.
G N. E. Purcell, Retail Meat Dealer.
H E. G. Austin, Barber Shop & Billiard Room.
I W. W. Wellington, Physician & Surgeon.
J Albert Bunnell, Ice Dealer & Trucking.
K Frank Babcock, Livery Stable.
L Wm. Robinson, Pleasant View Fa
M Levi Bassett, Farmer.
N Terryville Hotel, Jos. C. Barthe
O Town Hall, Probate & Clerk's O
P Congregational Church.
Q Catholic Church.
R High & Graded Schools.
S Eagle Lock Co's Middle Reserve
T Height of Land 960 feet.

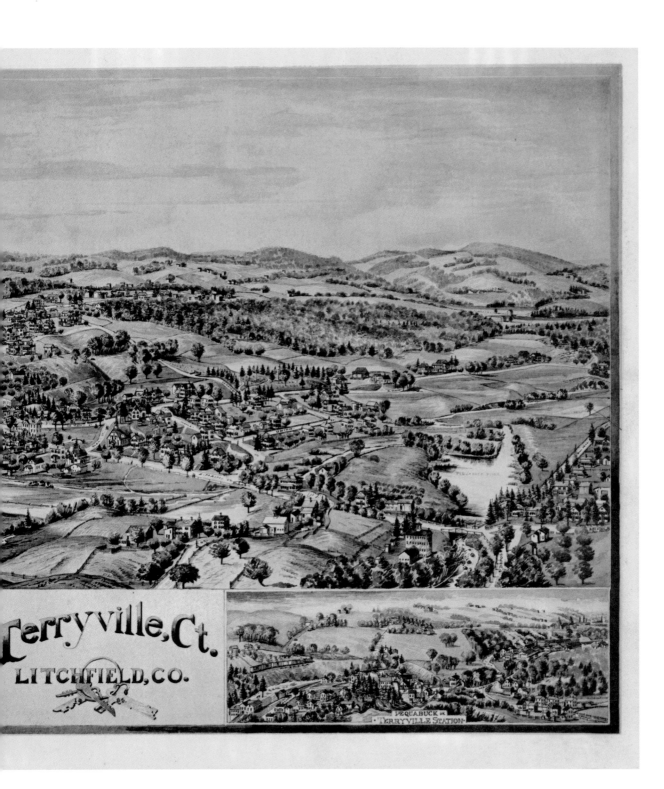

Terryville, Ct.
LITCHFIELD, CO.

PEQUABUCK &
TERRYVILLE STATION

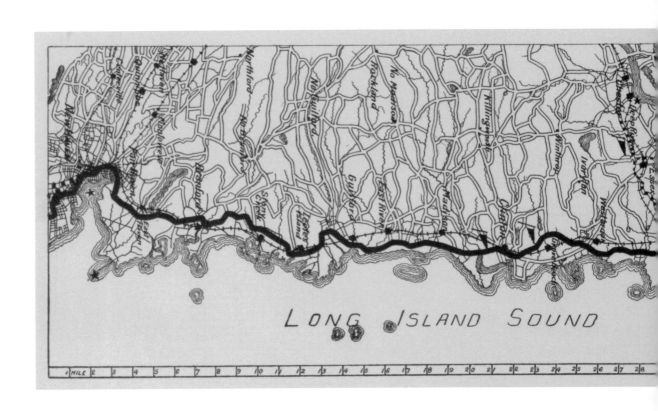

LONG ISLAND SOUND

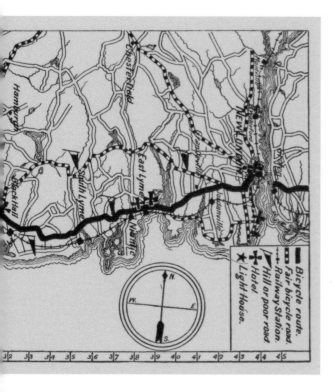

Bicycle Road Map. New Haven to New London—
Harper & Brothers (1895)
Bicycling was on the cutting edge of personal transportation in 1895. The first bicycles manufactured in America had been produced in a Hartford factory less than two decades earlier. This map alerts cyclists along the shoreline to the varying quality of the roads they can expect to encounter.

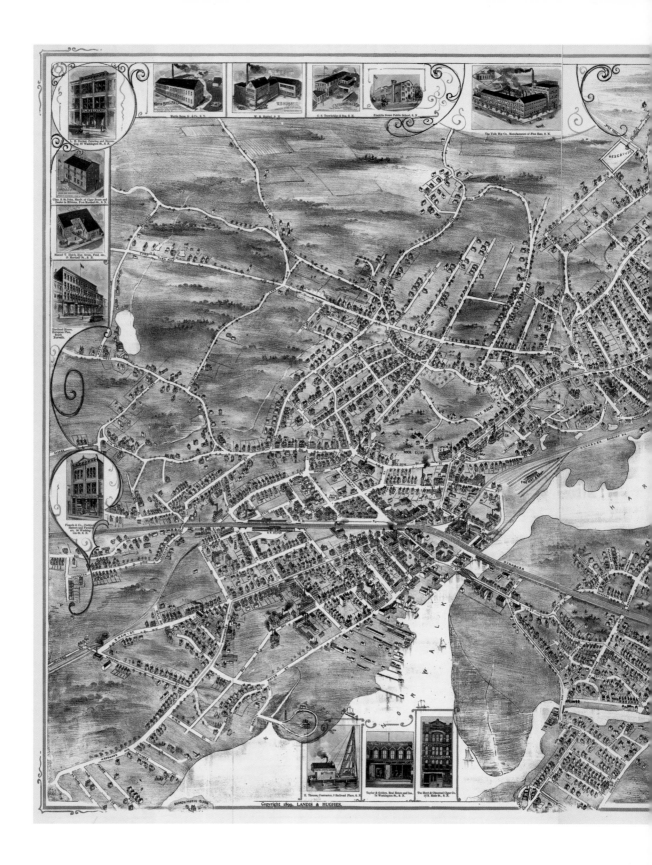

Copyright 1899, LANDIS & HUGHES.

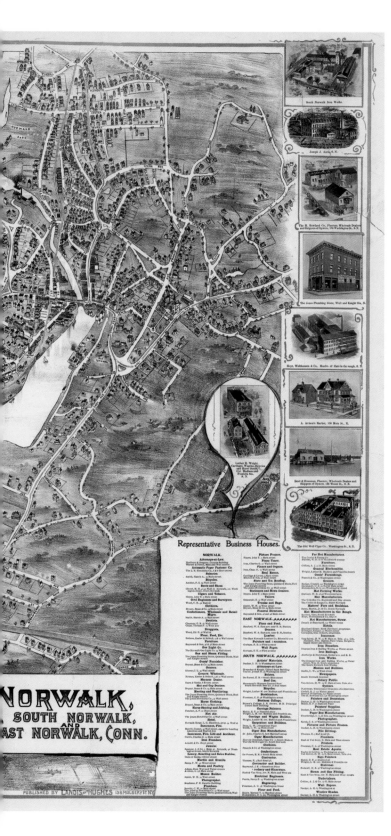

Norwalk, South Norwalk, and East Norwalk, Conn.—Landis and Hughes (1899)

Planting and harvesting oysters in Long Island Sound, located just off the bottom of this bird's-eye view, was a major economic activity in Norwalk at the turn of the twentieth century. The city's economic base was diversified, judging from the vignettes that surround the view, and included fashioning hats and making cigars.

Detail from map on pages 92 and 93

Twentieth and Twenty-first Centuries

THE EXPANSION OF INDUSTRY AND URBANIZATION and the influx of immigrants from an even wider assortment of foreign countries that had wrought profound changes on Connecticut in the last half of the nineteenth century continued into the twentieth century.

The Irish and Germans, who had been among the first immigrants to come to Connecticut in the mid-1800s, were joined by newcomers from more than two dozen other countries in the early 1900s. Countries from Armenia to Yugoslavia, from Greece to Russia sent significant numbers of immigrants to Connecticut. Of particular significance among the newcomers were the Italians, Poles, and French Canadians. The result was that by World War I, barely one in three Connecticut residents had been born in the United States.

Some of these new arrivals took up farming acres that had been left by discouraged Connecticut residents of previous generations. But the majority flocked to jobs in long-established industries and in new ones that were starting up as well.

Since factories were typically in cities, Connecticut was becoming an increasingly urban state. By 1910 more than 90 percent of Connecticut residents lived in a city. Living conditions could be grim in those cities for immigrants, who had brought little with them to their new home and worked at unskilled or semi-skilled work that might not pay very well. Often they were crowded into tenement buildings—either larger former residences transformed into apartments or structures hastily built to accommodate the influx of newcomers—that could be filthy, affording little light or fresh air, and offering inadequate sanitary facilities. Still they continued to come, fleeing poverty, oppression, or war in their native lands in the hope that the new country would offer something better.

Both World War I and World War II were boom years for Connecticut industry. Producing materials for the defense industry became an increasingly significant segment of the state's economic base. To the firearms and ammunition that had been manufactured since the early nineteenth century were added submarines in the early twentieth and helicopters in the mid-twentieth century.

The coming of the automobile to Connecticut in the early twentieth century brought changes every bit as profound and swift as those wrought by the railroad in the nineteenth. The number of cars in Connecticut increased from 40,000 in 1915 to 120,000 in 1920, a threefold increase in just five years. More than one in ten Connecticut residents owned a car.

Roads were improved to accommodate the ever-increasing number of automobiles on the road. The traffic congestion on the main two-lane road along the southwestern coastline grew so bad that the Merritt Parkway, a thirty-seven-mile-long, scenic limited-access divided highway from Greenwich to Stratford, was opened in 1940 to siphon off some of the excess automobiles.

Bridges were built to carry cars over major waterways. Bridges constructed across the Connecticut River prior to World War II included the Bulkeley Bridge in 1908 at Hartford; the "swing bridge" at East Haddam in 1913; and the Arrigoni Bridge at Middletown in 1938.

By 1950 Connecticut had two million residents. More than one quarter of them lived in one of four cities: Hartford, New Haven, Bridgeport, and Waterbury. But forces and features, some already in play, some new, would combine to reverse many of the trends and developments of the previous century, once again transforming the map of Connecticut.

The rapid rise in the birth rate—the post-war "baby boom"—that resulted when couples who had put starting or adding to their families on hold until the end of World War II, hit Connecticut hard. Between 1950 and 1970, the state's population increased by 50 percent.

Many of these new families were eager to get out of the crowded cities with their noise, smog, cramped quarters, and gritty atmosphere. That opportunity came with a flurry of road construction from the 1950s through the 1990s,

including numerous high-speed limited-access highways, some part of the Interstate Highway System. In some spots where the terrain was particularly hilly, routes were blasted or even tunneled through.

The affordability of automobiles, the new and improved roads and highways that made it possible to cover long distances in a short period of time, and the seemingly inexhaustible supply of cheap gasoline meant that workers were no longer tethered to the end of a rail line or trolley track. How far one lived from where one worked was determined only by how long a commute one was willing to make.

Within a few decades the trend that had dominated Connecticut for more than a century was reversed. As cities like Hartford, Bridgeport, and New Haven lost population, towns within convenient commuting distance to them by car saw sharp increases in population, doubling, tripling, or even more in just a couple of decades. As those towns closest to major employment centers began to fill up, rural communities that had been bypassed by trains, superhighways, and industry began to attract commuters. Connecticut was transformed within a generation or two into a land dominated by suburbs. Some of the historic fabric of towns was lost.

The cities suffered a second blow with the decline of industry in the latter part of the twentieth century. Manufacturers like the Collinsville Ax Company in Canton, the American Thread Company in Willimantic, Cheney Brothers Silk Mills in Manchester, and Yale & Towne Locks in Stamford, which had been in operation for well over a century, closed their doors. Some moved operations to less costly locations for manufacturing; others were worn down by the high cost of fuel or inability to compete with producers in less expensive locations.

Connecticut's economic base shifted from manufacturing to service industries, corporate headquarters, education, pharmaceutical research, and tourism. This last received a significant boost from the most unexpected of sources: the Pequot and Mohegan tribes.

Small numbers of both native peoples had managed to hold onto the fraction of their ancestral lands that had been set aside for them as reservations. In 1983 the Pequots received federal recognition as a sovereign nation. The Mohegans did the same in 1994. This allowed each tribe to build on their reservations casinos and entertainment complexes that attract thousands of visitors each year and generate millions in income for the state government.

RESIDENCE OF A. E. HAMMER.

RESIDENCE AND OFFICE OF DR. C. W. GAYLORD.

TRINITY EPISCOPAL CHURCH.

BRANFORD HIGH SCHOOL.

BLACKSTONE MEMORIAL LIBRARY.

FIRST CONGREGATIONAL CHURCH.

ST. MARY'S CATH

COPYRIGHT SECURED 1905 BY MOORES & BAILEY.

HOADLEY & HUTCHINSON'S BLOCK.

FRANK & STANNARD'S STORES, HOSLEY BLOCK.

P. JOURDAN & SON LUMBER AND COAL WHARF AND YARDS.

MALLEABLE IRON FITTING COMPANY'S MANUFACTORIES.

S. V. OSBORN, COAL AND LUMBER, GE

M. P. RICE'S STABLES.

BRAUN'S BAKERY. C. F. MEHT.

BIRD'S-EYE VIEW OF

BRANFORD,
CONNECTICUT.

MOORES & BAILEY, PUBLISHERS, 1905 15-17 GOLD STREET, NEW YORK.

Bird's-eye view of Branford, Connecticut—Hughes & Bailey (1905)

The shoreline town of Branford was a thriving community at the dawn of the twentieth century thanks to several factors. The Malleable Iron Fittings factory, established in 1854, offered employment to many individuals, including immigrants, as did several large quarries. Also, hotels to serve the needs of increasing numbers of summer vacationers were going up.

The jewel in the town's crown was the James Blackstone Memorial Library, depicted front and center at the top of the bird's-eye view. A grand building of Tennessee marble, it had been completed less than a decade earlier, in 1896, with a price tag of $300,000—the equivalent of more than $7 million today.

Aero view of New London, Connecticut—Hughes & Bailey (1911)

New London's heyday as a whaling port was only a memory by 1911, but ships and boats of all kinds were still prominent in just about every facet of life. Steamboats made regular runs from New York to New London, where passengers could switch to trains that would carry them anywhere they wished in New England. Both railroads and steamboat lines served the city's many industries as well.

Sailing ships plied the waters off New London for work and pleasure. The "boat race course" on the Thames River in the lower right of the view likely refers to the route of the Yale–Harvard Regatta, an annual race between the crew teams of the prestigious schools that attracted crowds of spectators.

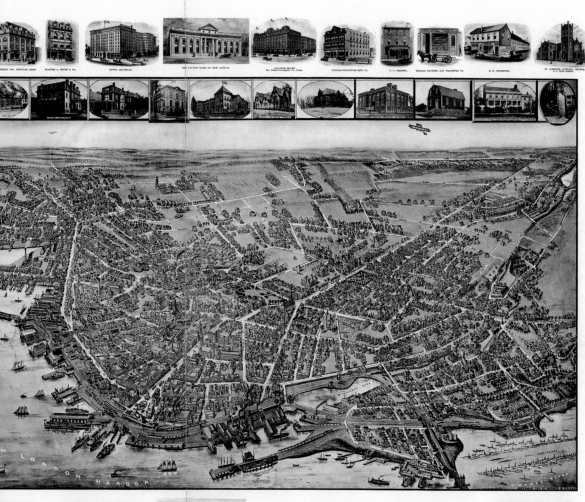

AERO VIEW OF
NEW LONDON
CONNECTICUT
1911

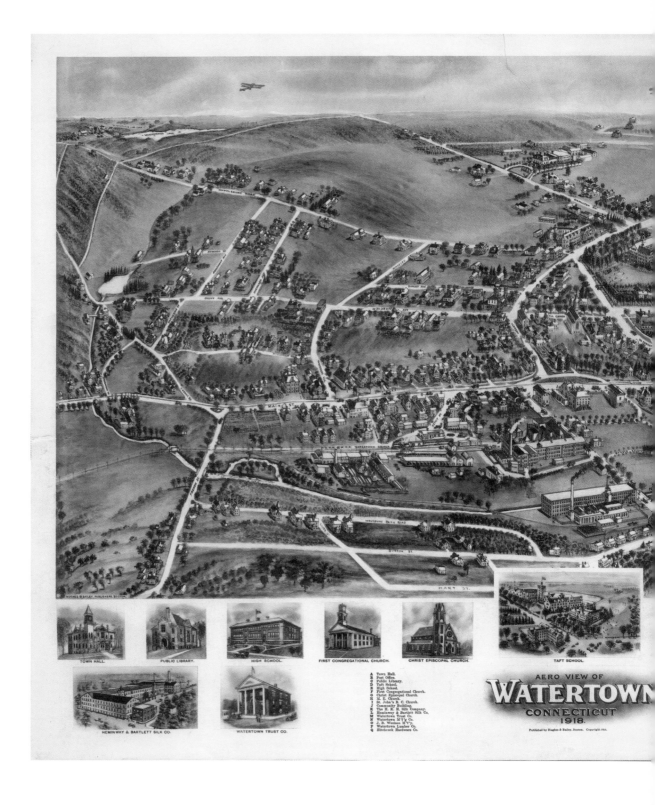

TOWN HALL. PUBLIC LIBRARY. HIGH SCHOOL. FIRST CONGREGATIONAL CHURCH. CHRIST EPISCOPAL CHURCH. TAFT SCHOOL.

HEMINWAY & BARTLETT SILK CO. WATERTOWN TRUST CO.

A Town Hall.
B Post Office.
C Public Library.
D Taft School.
E High School.
F First Congregational Church.
G Christ Episcopal Church.
H M. E. Church.
I St. John's R. C. Church.
J Community Building.
K The H. & B. Silk Company.
L Heminway & Bartlett Silk Co.
M Watertown Trust Co.
N Watertown M'f'g Co.
O J. B. Woolson M'f'y.
P Watertown Lumber Co.
Q Hitchcock Hardware Co.

AERO VIEW OF
WATERTOWN
CONNECTICUT
1918.

Published by Hughes & Bailey, Boston. Copyright 1918.

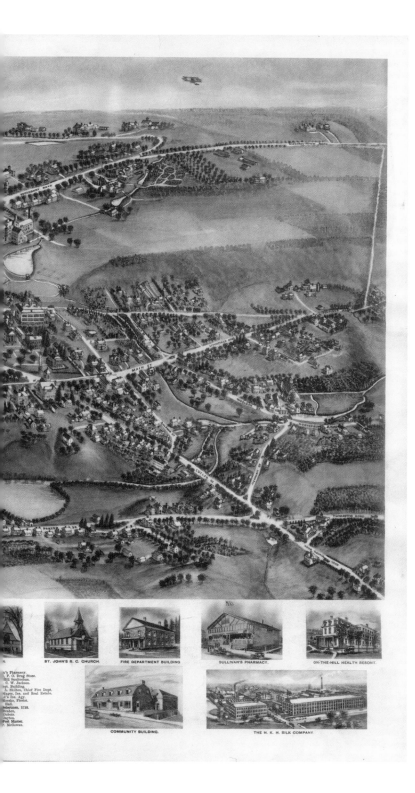

Aero view of Watertown, Connecticut—Hughes & Bailey (1918)

The manufacture of silk thread was a long-established major industry in Watertown by 1918. Silk is no longer made in Watertown, but the Taft School, founded in 1890 and featured prominently above the town's name on the bird's-eye view, still operates as one of the nation's elite prep schools.

City of Derby, Connecticut—Hughes & Bailey (1920)
By 1920 Derby, Connecticut, was flourishing as an industrial center thanks in large part to the Ousatonic Dam on the Housatonic River, only partly shown on the left edge of this view. The dam was built in 1870, turning the waters of the Housatonic into a source of power for factories that produced everything from corsets to pianos. At 5.3 square miles in size, Derby is the smallest town in Connecticut.

HUGHES & BAILEY, PUBLISHERS, 39-43 GOLD STREET, NEW YORK. COPYRIGHT 1920

CITY OF DERBY, CONNECTICUT

Modern Hotel, Opera House, Hospital, City Water Works, Gas and Electric Light and Power, Efficient Fire and Police Departments, Complete System of Sewers and Paved Streets, Public Parks, Golf Links and Country Club.

One of the Largest Water Powers in New England, Direct or Electrically applied, from the Ousatonic Dam. Also the Great New Water Power Plant at Stevenson is but nine miles distant.

Derby and its Sister City Shelton have a large number of Diversified Manufacturing Industries, including Rubber Mill Machinery, Iron and Brass Castings, Pianos and Piano Players, Tractors, Dairy Machinery, Corsets and Corset Accessories,

Pins, Machinery and Tools, Hosiery, Brass and Copper Goods, Webbing, Brass and Steel Wire Goods, Table Cutlery, Cotton Goods, Bolts and Rivets, Tacks, Buttons, Crucibles, Brass and Iron Bedsteads, Silk Plush and Velvets, and a variety of other products.

The many Natural Advantages of Location, the Cheapness of Power, Varied Industries, Skilled Labor, Facilities for Transportation, Proximity to other Large Manufacturing Communities combine to make Derby Exceptionally Attractive to the Manufacturer and Home Seeker as a Commercial and an Industrial Center.

Aero view of Ansonia, Connecticut—
Hughes & Bailey (1921)

Ansonia was settled in the late 1600s, but its transformation into an urban manufacturing center began in 1844. In that year industrialist Anson Greene Phelps began developing the area, which was then part of the town of Derby.

The town's name was suggested in 1845 by local physician Dr. Ambrose Beardsley. Phelpsville had been suggested as the name for the new community, but rejected, supposedly because Anson Phelps already had given that name to the site of another of his enterprises. Dr. Beardsley suggested that Phelps take his first name, "and make a Latin name of it and call it Ansonia; this will be euphonious, rather poetical, and will carry your name down to the latest generation." Anson Phelps died in 1853, but as Dr. Beardsley predicted, more than 150 years later he continues to be immortalized in the town's name.

Ansonia was incorporated from Derby as a town in 1889. By the time this bird's-eye view was printed in 1921, its factories were producing everything from brass to lace.

Connecticut: MAPPING THE NUTMEG STATE THROUGH HISTORY

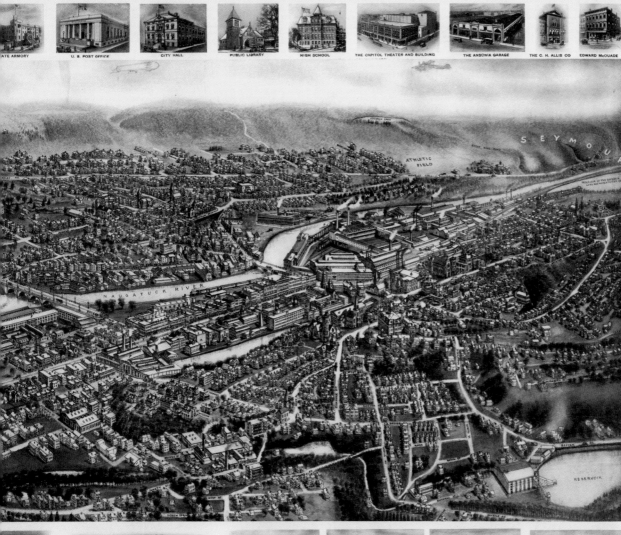

ATE ARMORY   **U. S. POST OFFICE**   **CITY HALL**   **PUBLIC LIBRARY**   **HIGH SCHOOL**   **THE CAPITOL THEATER AND BUILDING**   **THE ANSONIA GARAGE**   **THE C. H. ALLIS CO**   **EDWARD McQUADE**

SEYMOUR

ATHLETIC FIELD

NAUGATUCK RIVER

RESERVOIR

AERO VIEW OF
ANSONIA
CONNECTICUT
1921.

H. C. COOK CO

THE ANSONIA FLOUR AND GRAIN CO

R. J. HALL

THE S. O. & C. COMPANY

NORTH MAIN ST. (SECTION)

Central Market, Jacob Lacy, Prop., Cor. Main and Bridge Sts. Tel. 676.

Circuth, Isidor. 129 North State St., Confectionery and Cigars.

Cohen, S. Howard, Dr. Dental Surgeon. Main and Bridge Sts.

Cohen, Franklin, W. Attorney and Counselor at Law, 344 Main St.

Cohen, Dr. H. A. Optometrist.

Cook, H. C. Co., The. Sheet and Metal Novelties, Beaver Ave.

Comstock, G. A. Jeweler and Optometrist, 176 Main St.

Cottage Ave. Green Houses. J. W. Willis, Prop. 31 Cottage Ave.

Cressman, H. A. Real Estate and Insurance. 361 Main St.

Donovan Co., C. P. Dry Goods, Art Goods, Picture Framing, Capital Building.

Davis Drug Co. Registered Pharmacists, 169 North Main St.

Dwyer, F. S., Dr. Dentist, 129 Main St.

Evening Sentinel, The. Emerson Publishing Co., Inc., Prop'rs., 241 Main St.

"Fashion," The. S. F. Prigerson, 126 Main St.

Farrel Foundry & Machine Co. Est. 1848. Manufacturers of Chilled Rolls, Rubber and Sugar Machinery, Paper Calenders and Heavy Machinery.

Fasdis, H. G. Dealer in Dodge Brothers' Motor Cars. 166-164 Central Ave.

Fountain Water Company, The. Edwin D. Gager, Pres., Arthur L. Flak, Sec'y-Treas. Samuel J. Kyle, Supt. 21 Franklin St.

Gaffney, William. Plumber and Gas Fitter, Steam and Hot Water Heating Engineer, Tin and Sheet Iron Worker, 3 Church St., West Side.

Gardella, Geo. Fruit and Confectionery, 46 Main St.

Gillie, John. Dealer in Choice Groceries, 85 Franklin St.

Goodman, Henry H. Gen. Insurance and Real Estate, 218 Main St.

Gordy & Co., E. S. Gen. Insurance. Agent for all Leading Companies. Manager for Connecticut, The Fidelity Mutual Life Insurance Co., Opera House Block.

Hall, R. J. Contractor and Builder, 7 Lester Court.

Henry, J. F. Tools and Machinery, Holbrook Court.

Hine, Thomas J. Cigar Manufacturer, 29 Platt St.

Hutchins, Lockwood. Hardware, Paints and Oils, 152 Main St.

Isbell, Milton C. Attorney at Law, Goodalglot, 160 Main St.

Jacobson, J. E. Electrical Contractor. Fans, Motors and Fixtures, House and Bell Wiring a Specialty. 220 Westfield Ave.

Jenkins, Wm. H. Undertaker and Funeral Director, 8 Maple St.

Kennedy, John F. Cigars and Confectionery, 162 Main St.

Keegan, Thomas J. Dentist, Capitol Building.

Lattanzia, James. Photographer, Photo Supplies, Picture Framing, 13 Bridge St.

Lear Bros. Druggists, 68 Main St.

Legg, Thos. G., Dr. Surgeon Dentist, 2 Maple St.

Lundgren, A. P. Choice Groceries, Cor. Wakelee Ave. and Scotland St.

Malapolsy, M. D. New and old barrels, house, packing cases, Cooperage Stock, 167 Wakelee Ave.

Manfreal, Rev. P. L., Pastor Holy Rosary Church, 422 Main St.

Manufacturers' Club. Terry Building, 76 Main St.

Mead, J. C. Cooperage, 11 Elm St.

McCabe, Thomas F. Painter and Decorator, 18 Murray St.

McCarthy, Frederick M. Attorney at Law, 212 Main St.

McQuade, Edward. Ph. G. "The Prescription Man," 36 Main St.

Naugatuck Valley Morris Plan Bank. 59 Main St.

New York Plumbing Supply Co. Chas. Miller, Prop. Plumbing, Steam and Gas Fitting. 270 Main St.

Nixon & Carroll. Men's and Boys' Outfitters. Clothing, Furnishings, 174 Main St.

Palace of Sweets, The. Valerios Bros., Fine Confectionery, 212 Main St.

P. R. Tire Repair Shop. C. P. Palmer. Retreading and Vulcanizing, Auto Accessories. 174 No. Main, Cor. Fourth St.

Presco Undertaking Co., The.

Puritan Restaurant. 104 Main St.

Rowana, A. Groceries and Meats. 189 No. Main St.

Rubin's Sons. Vols. Iron and Metals, 449 Main St.

Savings Bank of Ansonia, The. William A. Nelson, Pres'd, Frederick T. Reitz, Treas. 117 Main St.

Schatz, August & Co. Painter and Decorator, 19 Lester St.

Scully Bros. Meats, Fish and Vegetables, 161 No. State St.

Smith, S. W. & Co. Apothecaries, 163 Main St.

Steeves, J. F. Grocer, 69 Cottage Ave.

S. O. & C. Co. Mfrs. of Eyelets and Eyelet Machinery, Canal St.

Spreutt, Rev. Joseph. Pastor Assumption Church, 25 No. Cliff St.

Terry & Son, T. P. Frank T. Terry, Proprietor. Hardware, Paints, Oils, Builders' and Factory Supplies, 76-80 Main St.

Tomlinson, Charles H. Jeweler and Optometrist, 146 Main St.

Worthington, William. Groceries and Provisions, 22 Clover St.

Woodford Tire & Supply Co. Truck and Pneumatic Tire Service Station, 169 Main St.

Welch & Son, Q. H. Staple and Fancy Groceries, 135 Main St.

Wentworth, Thos. U. Groceries and Provisions, 91 State St.

Wilhelm, William. Fancy and Pastry Baker. Wholesale and Retail Dealer in Flour, 389 Wakelee Ave., Cor. Gulf St.

Vavino, Frank. Deputy Sheriff. Real Estate and Insurance, 212 Main St.

COURTESY JAMES AND RUTH GOLDIE

Map of pioneer Hartford, founded 1636,
incorporated 1784, showing early landmarks
and the locations of historical events—
James and Ruth Goldie (1927)

This early twentieth-century version of "pioneer Hartford" combines whimsy, fact, imagination, nostalgic stereotypes, liberties with history—and several inaccuracies.

The only man-made feature on this map that survives to this day is the "Burial Ground"—today's Ancient Burying Ground. The Connecticut River was known as "Ye Great River" during the early years of settlement in acknowledgment of its size, especially in comparison to its tributary, "Ye Little River." The Little River, known sequentially as the Mill River, the Hog River, and the Park River, was channeled underground in the twentieth century as a flood-prevention measure.

The tree with the sheet of paper atop its leaves near the portrait of John Winthrop Jr. bears the explanation "The Charter was hidden in the oak on October 31, 1687." This was the famed "Charter Oak," in which legend says Connecticut's leaders hid the colony's Royal Charter of government to prevent a representative of the King of England from taking it back. Although the tree itself fell in the 1800s, an imposing stone pillar still marks its approximate location.

John Winthrop Jr., however, was not the first governor of Connecticut from 1635 to 1636. He didn't achieve that post until 1657.

The "Pequot Fort" shown at the lower left can only be intended to illustrate the pallisaded Pequot village at Mystic in southeastern Connecticut that was burned in the Pequot War in 1637. Even allowing the artists some artistic license in trying to show the fort on a map of Hartford, they erred in putting teepees like those occupied by Plains Indians inside the fort instead of the wigwams that were actually used by the Pequots.

Connecticut State Park Picture Plan—(1929)

By 1929 Connecticut had set aside more than 50,000 acres in state parks and forests. They ranged in size from a single acre to more than 7,600 acres and, as this map shows, the fifty-five sites were scattered all around the state.

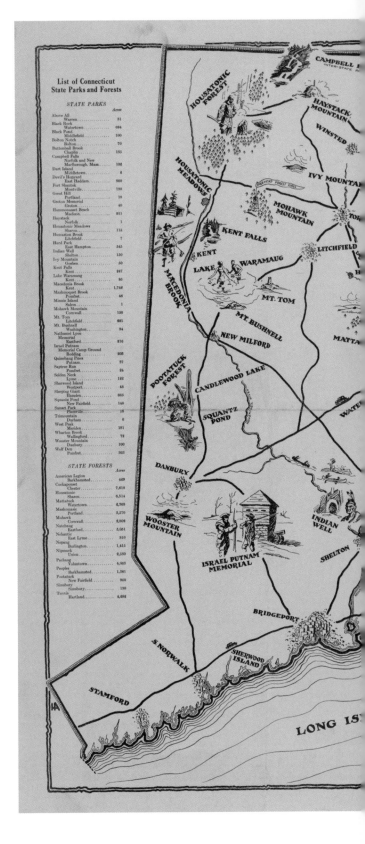

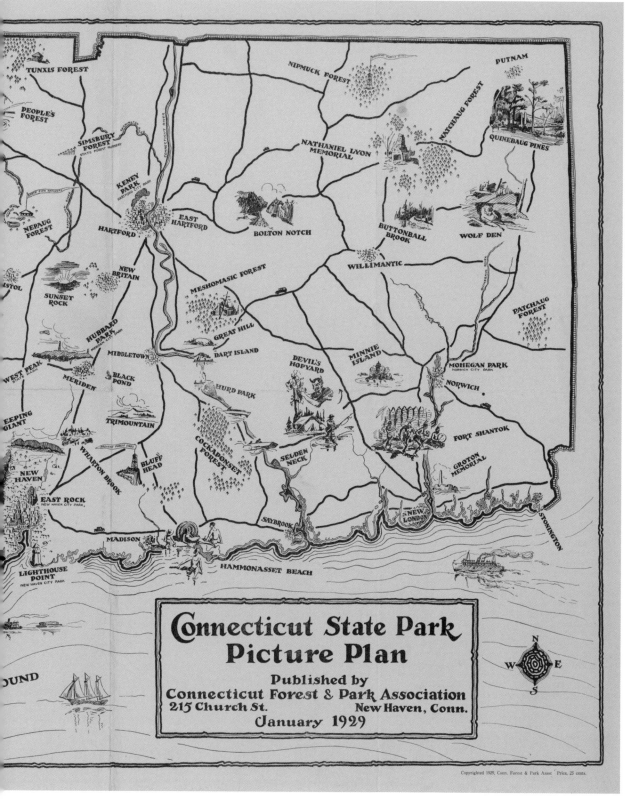

Connecticut State Park
Picture Plan
Published by
Connecticut Forest & Park Association
215 Church St.   New Haven, Conn.
January 1929

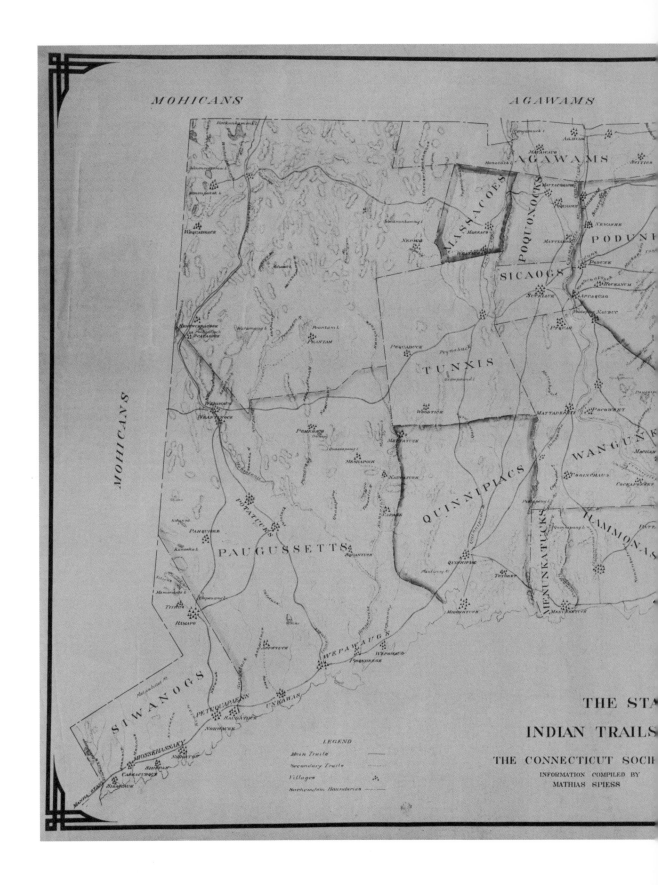

MOHICANS

AGAWAMS

MOHICANS

AGAWAMS

MASSACOES

POQUONOCKS

PODUNK

SICAOGS

TUNXIS

WANGUNK

PAUGUSSETTS

QUINNIPIACS

MENUNKATUCKS

HAMMONAS...

WEPAWAUGS

SIWANOGS

LEGEND

Main Trails
Secondary Trails
Villages
Sachemdom Boundaries

THE STA
INDIAN TRAILS
THE CONNECTICUT SOCI
INFORMATION COMPILED BY
MATHIAS SPIESS

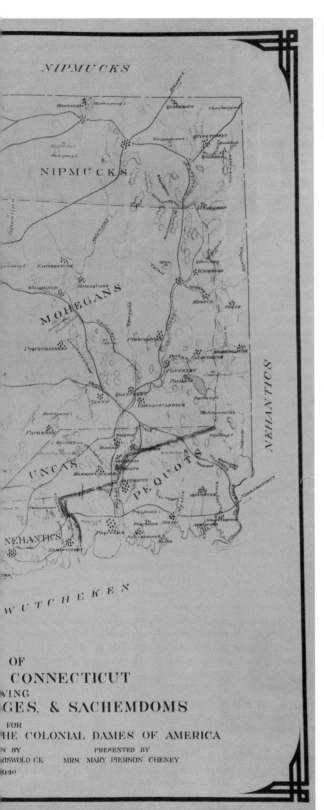

Map of the State of Connecticut Showing Indian Trails, Villages, and Sachemdoms—Griswold, Spiess (1930)

The trails, villages, and spheres of influence of more than a dozen native peoples prior to the arrival of Europeans in Connecticut are depicted in this 1930 map researched by Mathias Spiess.

Art and Architecture Building, Yale University, New Haven, Connecticut. Site plan including Church Street and museums—Rudolph (1961)

Architect Paul Rudolph's sketch of the site plan for Yale University's Art and Architecture Building only hints at the innovative Modernist design that would fuel controversy from the day it opened its doors in 1963. Rudolph's building applied the Brutalist design feature of rough-surfaced concrete construction, with square, blank-faced towers. Inside it was even more unconventional, with more than thirty different levels in a building only seven stories tall.

Architecture critic Michael Crosbie has called the Yale Art and Architecture Building "one of the most iconic architecture school buildings in the world. The structure," Crosbie claims, "made Rudolph one of the most famous architects of his time."

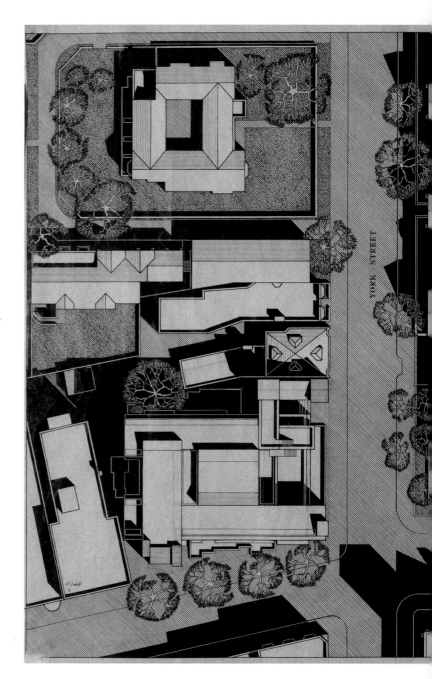

CHAPEL STREET

HIGH STREET

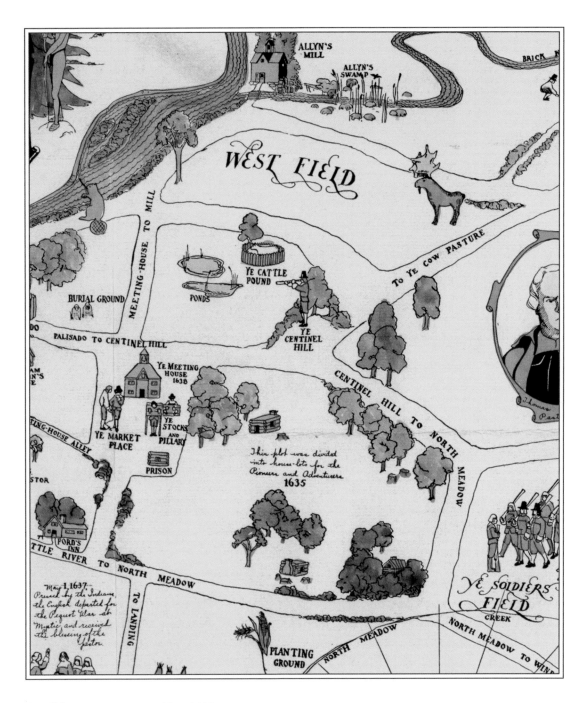

Detail from map on pages 102 and 103

Conclusion

CONNECTICUT IN THE SECOND DECADE OF THE twenty-first century is the product of repeated profound changes, including revolution, emigration, immigration, industrialization, and suburbanization, to name just a few. It faces the challenge of dealing effectively with the legacy of these changes and with the unlikely, but never impossible, chance that yet another unforeseen monumental development like those of the past will come along to reshape the state once more.

Maps, as marvelous and magical as they are, cannot reveal everything about a place. Some things became apparent only when one is on the ground. In Connecticut those include the abundance of historic structures that reflect life over the course of nearly four centuries.

Connecticut includes an abundance of historic districts, some encompassing a hundred buildings or more. A stroll down the streets of just about any of these enclaves can be a walk through time: small seventeenth-century saltboxes, finely adorned eighteenth-century Georgian mansions, nineteenth-century pillared and pedimented Greek Revival dwellings, twentieth-century subdivisions and workers' housing. Connecticut boasts renowned architectural gems from

the 1639 medieval-style Stone House in Guilford to the outlandishly lavish home of Mark Twain in Hartford to architect Philip Johnson's cleanly geometric and transparent 1949 Glass House in New Canaan.

Surviving structures bear witness to the world of work as well, from the massive Hartford Colt firearms factory with its startling blue star-spangled onion dome to the granite-block textile mills in Willimantic. Town greens speak of the central role that community played in the history of Connecticut towns from their very beginning. Meetinghouses, cathedrals, synagogues, and temples represent the diversity that has characterized Connecticut for nearly two centuries.

Graveyards with tombstones carved by skilled craftsmen express the challenges of existence two and three hundred years ago and the changing role of religion in coping with those challenges. Stone walls, often half hidden in overgrown lots that were once fields, speak of a time when farming the sometimes uncooperative land was the way of life for most.

After experiencing over the past century spurts of explosive growth, first from immigration and then the post–World War II "baby boom," Connecticut's population has become relatively stable in size. The state's population increased less than 4 percent between 1990 and 2000, while the number of people in the United States as a whole increased 13 percent. Connecticut's population is expected to have increased approximately 3.3 percent between 2000 and 2010, to a bit more than 3.5 million people.

The rush to the suburbs in the last decades of the twentieth century has slowed but not stopped. The transformation of villages into suburbs seemingly overnight has lost some momentum as well. But expansion of homes and businesses into undeveloped areas still continues at a significant rate. "Sprawl" has entered the vocabulary of citizens and policymakers alike, concerned with balancing residential and economic growth with the need to bring some cohesiveness to communities and to preserve both natural and man-made features that embody Connecticut's heritage.

Packing 3.5 million inhabitants into approximately 5,000 square miles has resulted in a population density in Connecticut of more than 700 people per square mile. That makes it the fourth densest state in the nation.

Yet that statistic is deceiving, for Connecticut is not primarily an urban state. One of the ironies in the change in Connecticut's landscape is how nature has slowly reclaimed so much of it. In 1895 only one-fifth of Connecticut's land was forested, the other four-fifths having been cleared for communities and, most prominently, fields to farm. A little more than a century later, the number of acres of forest land in Connecticut has tripled, as trees grew anew on abandoned farmland.

Today Connecticut is one of the most densely forested of the fifty states. That includes more than one hundred state parks and forests, as well as thousands of acres preserved by the state, towns, and private trusts as open space.

With the return of the forest have come wild animals rarely, if ever, seen in Connecticut during the last two centuries. White-tailed deer abound, while black bears have been sighted in more than one hundred Connecticut towns. The excited gobbling of turkeys early in the morning is a common sound at certain times of the year, as is the crazed yipping of packs of coyotes at night.

Mapmakers of the coming decades will likely have little need to change any of the state's man-made boundaries. Connecticut has 169 towns. The last one was created in 1921, and despite occasional grumbling from residents of a section of one town or another about breaking away to claim independent status, the likelihood of a 170th town forming anytime soon seems slim. Some towns perpetuate the time-honored tradition of regularly "perambulating" the boundaries, in which the first selectmen (the equivalent of the mayors) of adjoining municipalities walk their common border, making sure that markers are in their proper places.

Those 169 towns embody some of the most fundamental qualities of Connecticut that must be balanced with the challenges of the twenty-first century. Each town manages its own civic affairs, and in most cases even operates its own school system. Many residents cherish that quality of local self-determination that has its roots in the 1600s.

But in a twenty-first-century world, when more people than ever before require or demand increasing levels of service from their communities, and the cost of just about everything con-

Connecticut: Mapping the Nutmeg State through History

tinues to rise relentlessly, maintaining that degree of autonomy is becoming ever more difficult. Some towns have organized to share resources, and there exist in the state more than a dozen regional school districts, each of which serves two or more towns. But the concept of more aggressive regionalization that would require towns to relinquish some control over their affairs has been slow to gain acceptance.

The state's greatest waterway, the Connecticut River, still serves as a cultural dividing line, with New York exerting influence west of the river and Boston on the east, just as it did more than two centuries ago. While the opposing viewpoints held today on opposite banks of the river concern issues far less vital than those that separated Loyalists and patriots during the American Revolution, the passion can sometimes be just as fierce. For the Connecticut River is the de facto line of demarcation between New York Yankees fans to the west and Boston Red Sox fans to the east.

Acknowledgments

First on the list is Erin Turner, whose vision and creative editorial participation make these books a joy for me; without her this audacious project would not be the permanent achievement it is destined to be. On our Globe Pequot Press team I treasure Julie Marsh (indefatigable project manager), Sheryl Kober (visionary designer—oh, these vellum jackets!), Lori Enik (digital file miracle worker), and Casey Shain (layout artist). The patience, organizational skills, and technical wizardry of my gifted colleague Aimee Hess are essential to my survival, as is the research assistance I receive from the masters in the Library of Congress Geography and Map Division: John Hebert (its chief), Cynthia Cook, John Hessler, Charlotte Houtz, Michael Klein, Stephen Paczolt, and Edward Redmond.

—VINCENT VIRGA

My thanks go to Erin Turner, who provided me with the opportunity to be part of this ambitious project, and to Julie Marsh, who skillfully shepherded the book through editing and production.

—DIANA ROSS MCCAIN

All maps come from Library of Congress Geography and Map Division Washington, D.C. 20540-4650 unless otherwise noted. To order reproductions of Library of Congress items, please contact the Library of Congress Photoduplication Service, Washington, D.C., 20540-4570 or (202) 707-5640.

Page ii Novi Belgii Novæque Angliæ: nec non partis Virgininiæ tabula multis in locis emendata; per Nicolaum Visscher nunc apud Petr. Schenk Iun, 1685. G3715 169- .V5 TIL Vault.

Page viii Ruysch, Johann. Universalior cogniti orbis tabula. In Claudius Ptolemeus, *Geographia.* Rome, 1507. G1005.1507 Vault.

Page ix Waldseemüller, Martin. Universalis cosmographia secundum Ptholomaei traditionem et Americi Vespucii alioru que lustrations. St. Dié, France?, 1507. G3200 1507 .W3 Vault.

Page 4 Avery, Humphry. A plan of the lands in New London sequestred for the sole use and improvement of the Mohegan Indian tribe, survey'd and measured the 7th, 8th & 9th of Septr. 1736 and protracted by the above scale of 60 pts. to an inch by me, Humphry Avery, survr, for the county of New London, 1736. G3784.M73G46 1736 .A9 Vault.

Pages 8–9 The figure of the Indians' fort or palizado in New England and the manner of the destroying it by Captayne Underhill and Captayne Mason, RH., 1638. Illus. in: Nevves from America, by John Underhill. London: Printed by J.D. for Peter Cole, 1638. Rare Book and Special Collections Division, Library of Congress. E83.63 .U55. Copy negative number LC-USZ62-32055 in Prints and Photographs Division, Library of Congress.

Page 10 Kitchin, Thomas. A map of the colonies in Connecticut and Rhode Island, divided by counties & townships, from best authorities. London, 1758. G3780 1758 .K5 TIL Vault.

Pages 14–15 Park, Moses. To the right honourable, the Earl of Shelbourne, His Majesty's principal Secretary of State for the Southern Department. This plan of the colony of Connecticut in North-America. Is humbly dedicated by his lordships most obedient humble servt. Moses Park. Novr. 24, 1766. G3780 1766 .P3 Vault.

Pages 16–17 Gibson, J[ohn]. A new and accurate map of part of North-America, comprehending the provinces of New England, New York, Pensilvania, New Jersey, Connecticut, Rhode Island & part of Virginia, Canada and Hallifax, for the illustration of Mr. Peter Kalms travels. London?, 1771. G3710 1771 .G5 Vault.

Pages 18–19 Huyser, C. J. de. Nieuwe en nauwkeurige kaart van een gedeelte van Noord Amerika, behelzende Nieuw Engeland, New York, Pensylvania, New Jersey, Connecticut, Rhode Island, een stuk van Virginia, Kanada en Halifax, ter opheldering der reizen van den Heer P. Kalm. P. Mol, geletterdt. Utrecht, J. v. Schoonhoven & Comp. en G. v. d. Brink Jz, 1772. G3710 1771 .H91 Vault.

Pages 24–25 A map of Connecticut and Rhode Island with Long Island Sound, &c. London, 1776. G3780 1776 .M2 TIL Vault.

Page 26 Gov. Tryon's expedition to Danbury, 1777. G3784.D2S3 1777 .G6 Vault.

Page 27 Campaign of MDCCLXXVI. London?, 1780? G3791.S3 1780 .C3 Vault : Roch 24.

Pages 28–29 Marche de l'armée française de Providence à la Rivière du Nord, 1781. G3711.S3 1781 .M3 Vault : Roch 42.

Page 30 Lyman, Daniel. A sketch of New London & Groton with the attacks made on Forts Trumbull & Griswold by the British troops under the command of Brigr. Genl. Arnold, Sept. 6th. 1781. G3784.N5S3 1781 .L9 Faden 98.

Page 31 Fort-Griswold, 1781? G3784.N5:2F6S3 1781 .F6 Faden 99.

Pages 32–33 (detail, page 20) France, Dépôt des cartes et plans de la marine. Carte générale de l'Océan Atlantique ou Occidental, dressée au Dépôt général des cartes, plans, et journaux de la marine, et publiée par ordre du Ministre pour le service des vaisseaux français en 1786. 5. éd., revue et corrigée en 1792, l'an 1er. de la République. Paris, 1792. G9110 1792 .F7 Vault: Roch 1.

Pages 34-35 Soulés, François. Differents camps de l'armée de York-town à Boston. Paris, 1787. G3701. S3 1787 .S6 Vault : Roch 64.

Pages 36–37 Doolittle, Amos. Connecticut, from the best authorities. Philadelphia?, 1795? G3780 1795 .D6 Vault : Roch 7.

Pages 42–43 Melish, John Græme. Geographical conversation cards: states of the United States. New York: A.T. Goodrich, 1824 (Clayton & Van Norden, printers). G3701.A9 svar .M4 Vault Shelf.

Pages 44–45 (detail, page 38) Young, J. H. Map of Massachusetts, Connecticut and Rhode Island; constructed from the latest authorities. Philadelphia, 1831. G3720 1831 .Y6 RR 97.

Pages 46–47 Anderson, P. Map exhibiting the experimental and located lines for the New-York and New-Haven Rail-Road. Projected and drawn by P. Anderson, civil engr. New York: Snyder & Black Lithogrs., 1845. G3801.P3 1845 .A5 RR 484.

Pages 48–49 L'Amérique centr[ale], I jou [?], Henri II, Mr. Jomard, ca. 1850. G3300 1542 .A5 Vault.

Pages 50–51 Williams, Alexander. Telegraph and Rail Road map of the New England States. Boston, 1854. G3721.P3 1854 .W5 RR 109.

Page 52 Woodford, E. M. Smith's map of Hartford County, Connecticut, 1855. G3783.H3G46 1855 .W6 TIL.

Page 53 Hopkins, G. M. Clark's map of Litchfield County, Connecticut, 1859. G3783.L5 1859 .H6 TIL.

Pages 54–55 Map showing the line of the Connecticut & Western Railroad and its connections. New York: G.W. & C.B. Colton & Co., 1871. G3716.P3 1871 .G15 RR 390.

Pages 56–57 View of New Britain, Conn. 1875. Lithography by C.H. Vogt, printing by J. Knauber & Co. Boston: O.H. Bailey & Co., 1875. G3784.N3A3 1875 .B3.

Pages 58–59 View of Bridgeport, Ct. 1875. O.H. Bailey & Co. Milwaukee: American Oleograph Co., 1875. G3784.B7A3 1875 .B3.

Pages 60–61 Birmingham, Conn. 1876. Boston: O.H. Bailey & Co., 1876. G3784.B54A3 1876 .B3.

Pages 62–63 View of Rockville, Conn. 1877. Lithography and printing by J. Knauber & Co., Milwaukee, Wisconsin. O.H. Bailey & Co., 1877. G3784.R7A3 1877 .B3.

Pages 64–65 View of Windsor Locks, Conn. 1877. Lithography & printing by J. Knauber & Co., Milwaukee, Wisconsin. Boston: O.H. Bailey & Co., 1877. G3784.W82A3 1877 .B3.

Pages 66–67 View of Stafford Springs, Conn. 1878. Boston: O.H. Bailey & Co., 1878. G3784.S68A3 1878 .B3.

Pages 68–69 Bailey, O. H. View of Mystic River & Mystic Bridge, Conn. 1879. Boston: Drawn & pub. by O. H. Bailey & J. C. Hazen, 1879. G3784.M92A3 1879 .B3.

Pages 70–71 View of Clinton, Connecticut 1881. Boston: O.H. Bailey & Co., 1881. G3784.C4A3 1881 .B3.

Pages 72–73 View of Essex, Centerbrook & Ivoryton, Conn. 1881. Boston: O.H. Bailey & Co., 1881. G3784.E85A3 1881 .B3.

Page 74–75 View of Cheshire, Connecticut 1882. Boston: O.H. Bailey & Co., 1882. G3784.C29A3 1882 .O2.

Pages 76–77 Hart, Charles, lithographer. Willimantic, Conn., 1882: From Blake Mountain, Wils Porter del.; Charles Hart, Lith. New York, New York: W.O. Laughna, Art Publishing Co., 1882. Prints and Photographs Division, Library of Congress. LC-DIG-pga-01486.

Pages 78–79 Burleigh, L. R. Stamford, Conn. Milwaukee: Beck & Pauli Lith., 1883. G3784.S7A3 1883 .B8.

Pages 80–81 Norris, George E. Bristol, Conn. looking north-east. Burleigh Lith. Est. Brockton, Mass., 1889. G3784.B8A3 1889 .N6.

Pages 82–83 Norris, George E. Terryville, Ct., Litchfield Co. Brockton, Mass., 1894? G3784.T4A3 1894 .N6.

Pages 84–85 Bicycle Road Map. New Haven, Connecticut, to New London, Connecticut. New York: Harper & Brothers, 1895.

Pages 86–87 Norwalk, South Norwalk, and East Norwalk, Conn. New York: Landis and Hughes, 1899. G3784.N7A3 1899 .L3.

Pages 92–93 (detail, page 88) Bird's-eye view of Branford, Connecticut. New York: Hughes & Bailey, 1905. G3784.B599A3 1905 .H8.

Pages 94–95 Aero view of New London, Connecticut 1911. New York: Hughes & Bailey, 1911. G3784.N5A3 1911 .H8.

Pages 96–97 Aero view of Watertown, Connecticut 1918. Boston: Hughes & Bailey, 1918. G3784.W329A3 1918 .H8.

Pages 98–99 City of Derby, Connecticut. New York: Hughes & Bailey, 1920. G3784.D7A3 1920 .H8 Fow 81.

Pages 100–101 Aero view of Ansonia, Connecticut 1921. Waterbury, Conn.: Hughes & Bailey, 1921. G3784.A6A3 1921 .H8.

Pages 102–3 (detail, page 110) Goldie, James and Ruth. Map of pioneer Hartford: founded 1636, incorporated 1784, showing early landmarks and the locations of historical events, 1927. G3784.H3 1927 .G6.

Pages 104–5 Connecticut State Park Picture Plan. New Haven, Connecticut: Connecticut Forest and Park Association, 1929.

Pages 106–7 Map of the State of Connecticut Showing Indian Trails, Villages, and Sachemdoms. Made for The Connecticut Society of the Colonial Dames of America. Information compiled by Mathias Spiess. Drawn by Hayden L. Griswold C.E. Presented by Mrs. Mary Pierson Cheney. Copyright 1859, pub. 1930.

Pages 108–9 Rudolph, Paul, architect. Art and Architecture Building, Yale University, New Haven, Connecticut. Site plan including Church Street and museums, 1961. Prints and Photographs Division, Library of Congress. LC-DIG-ppmsca-19114.

About the Authors

VINCENT VIRGA earned critical praise for *Cartographia: Mapping Civilization* and coauthored *Eyes of the Nation: A Visual History of the United States* with the Library of Congress and Alan Brinkley. Among his other books are *The Eighties: Images of America*, with a foreword by Richard Rhodes; *Eisenhower: A Centennial Life*, with text by Michael Beschloss; and *The American Civil War: 365 Days*, with Gary Gallagher and Margaret Wagner. He has been hailed as "America's foremost picture editor" for having researched, edited, and designed nearly 150 picture sections in books by authors including John Wayne, Jane Fonda, Arianna Huffington, Walter Cronkite, Hillary Clinton, and Bill Clinton. Virga edited *Forcing Nature: Trees in Los Angeles*, photographs by George Haas for Vincent Virga Editions. He is the author of six novels, including *Gaywyck*, *Vadriel Vail* and *A Comfortable Corner*, as well as publisher of ViVa Editions. He has a Web site through the Author's Guild at www.vincentvirga.com.

DIANA ROSS McCAIN has been writing about Connecticut's past for more than twenty-five years. She is the author of three books published by Globe Pequot Press: *It Happened in Connecticut; Connecticut Coast;* and *Mysteries and Legends of New England*. She also wrote the award-winning publication *To All on Equal Terms*, the story of Connecticut's official state heroine, Prudence Crandall. McCain holds bachelor's and master's degrees in history. She is Head of the Research Center at the Connecticut Historical Society in Hartford. She lives in Durham, Connecticut.